RIPSNORTING WHOPPERS!

For Michelle
and Alyssa...

[signature]

6/18/01

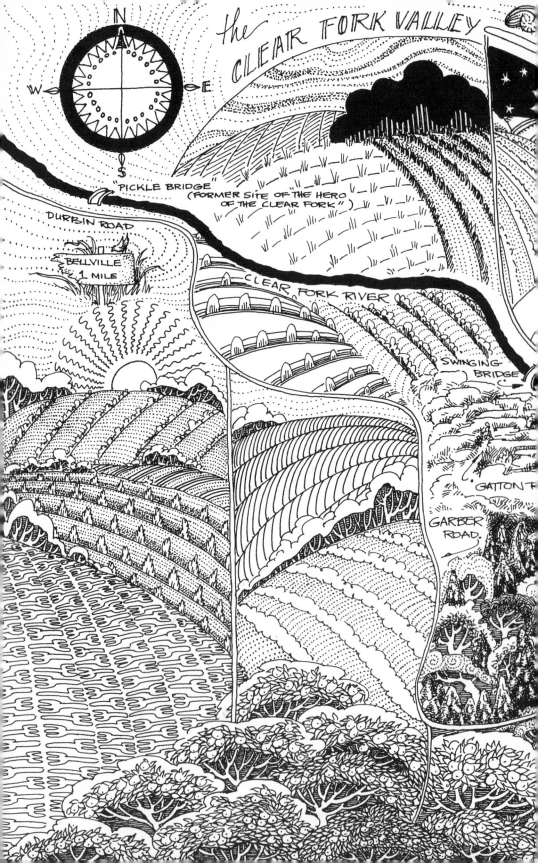

RIPSNORTING WHOPPERS!

Humor from America's Heartland

Rick Sowash

Illustrated by Maureen O'Keefe

Gabriel's Horn
Publishing Co.

Bowling Green, Ohio

About the Cover:

Here we see young Cy Gatton in desperate straits, nearly overwhelmed by the stunning results of his daring to plant the first seed—it happened to be a cucumber seed—ever planted in the most fer-tile soil in Richland County, Ohio.

About the Frontispiece:

The map shows the portion of the Clear Fork Valley in which most of Cy Gatton's adventures took place. The Clear Fork River runs right through the middle of the Gatton farm, today the Wade & Gatton Nursery. It is one of the five forks of the Mohican River, the watershed that forms north-central Ohio's fabled "Mohican Country."

Gabriel's Horn Publishing Co., Inc.
P.O. Box 141
Bowling Green, OH 43402
Editorial and business office: 419/352-1338
Orders only: 800/235-HORN (that's 4676)

Manufactured in the United States of America.

03 02 01

Softcover: 0-911861-07-6
Hardcover: 0-911861-08-4

Library of Congress Cataloging-in-Publication Data

Sowash, Rick.
　　Ripsnorting whoppers! : humor from America's heartland / Rick Sowash ; illustrated by Maureen O'Keefe.
　　　　p.　　cm.
　　Includes index.
　　ISBN 0-911861-08-4 : $19.95. -- ISBN 0-911861-07-6 (pbk.) : $11.95
　　1. Tall tales--Ohio.　2. Folklore--Ohio.　3. Tall tales--Middle West.　4. Folklore--Middle West.　5. Gatton, Cyrus Miller, 1863-1937.　I. Title.
GR110.O48S68　1994
398.2'09771--dc20
　　　　　　　　　　　　　　　　　　　　　　　　　94-29935
　　　　　　　　　　　　　　　　　　　　　　　　　CIP

Dedication

For the three people I love most:

my wife, Jo Anna Ackerman
my daughter, Shenandoah Lee
my son, John Chapman

I am a teller of tales—

tall ones, mostly—and I'm about to tell you some...in hopes of making you laugh, mostly. Our ancestors told these stories for fun, but there's something more than fun in them: they are a rambunctious celebration of the land, animals and people of America's Heartland. You might even call them secular hymns of praise.

So turn the pages and meet a genuine folk hero of the American Heartland: Cy Gatton. Cy was a real person and he told most of the stories I re-tell today. They are stories of his own supposed adventures, stories so pre-posterous and so vividly told that no one who heard them could ever recall them afterward without a smile.

They really are amazing stories.
Incredible stories.
Ripsnorting whoppers.

Rick Sowash

Contents

Foreword

by James Hope

I was blessed with a beguiling storyteller for a father. Night after night, when I was little, he told tales of the animal kingdom that thrived just outside our doors. He met its denizens—rabbits, skunks, woodchucks, foxes—on his way home from the office each evening, he said, and, like a good reporter, collected news and gossip from them for my entertainment (and, sometimes, moral instruction). I marvelled at all the creatures Dad knew on a first-name basis.

When I grew up and became a journalist, I found myself writing news articles by day and spinning tales by night for my four children. I began to see the similarities. The best news features—the real crowd pleasers and the ones my editors liked most—were the ones with novelty, drama, action, humor... the same qualities my young listeners at home demanded in their bedtime stories.

We never thought much about it, but my father and I were engaged in something both universal and eternal. Storytelling is one of the things that makes us human; it links us together around the world and, through folklore, maintains a vibrant thread of continuity with our past as well. And good storytellers do more than entertain: they help us remember who we are and how marvelous our world is.

That's quite a responsibility. But while all of us tell stories at one time or another, only a few are masters of the art. One of the masters is Rick Sowash, a native Ohioan and full-time professional storyteller whose tales have roots in the Heartland. Most of us get our entertainment by spinning television dials, but Rick spins his tales in person, one live audience at a time.

Perhaps just because this is an age of mass entertainment homogenized and canned by far-away dream factories, the up-close-and-personal teller of tales who can shower you with his sweat as well as his wit is enjoying a renaissance. Among the storytellers travelling the land, however, Rick Sowash is something special. Like other master storytellers, he can enthrall audiences, young and old. His stories have novelty, action, drama, and humor. He can spin tales that may startle you out of your chair one moment and have you shaking with laughter the next.

But Rick Sowash and his stories have something else. They have Cy Gatton.

Deep in the heart of Ohio, in the countryside Johnny Appleseed used to roam, Sowash has discovered and brought back to life a lost American folk hero. Cy Gatton, Sowash believes, is Ohio's answer to the likes of Mike Fink and Paul Bunyan. Formidable in mind, body and imagination, Gatton was a real person who grew up in the late 1800s and reached the peak of his storytelling powers early in this century. Like ancient storytellers, Gatton spun fabulous tales about his own adventures in farming, hunting and woods-walking. As Sowash does today, Gatton appealed to audiences young and old, the stories evoking in listeners of all ages that exquisite sense of wonder we assume we lost along with our childhoods. Wreathed in the charm of a more innocent and optimistic age, they are stories so amazing that...you just might call them tall tales.

Which is why Rick Sowash can rightly be called the "master of the tall tale." Cy Gatton may be gone, but he is not forgotten, as Rick Sowash brings his legend to life again...in person at appearances throughout the country, on audio and video tape, and, now, in this book. We have here an exuberant celebration of the American land, its people, places and creatures.

The art of the storyteller is written on the wind, and Rick Sowash never tells a story exactly the same way twice. We are fortunate to have captured one telling of his Cy Gatton stories...a treasure of witty, wise and wonderful Americana, masterfully told. You'll laugh and laugh.

And perhaps you'll discover your sense of wonder again.

(James Hope wrote, with Susan Failor, Bountiful Ohio: Good Food and Stories from Where the Heartland Begins.*)*

Acknowledgements

*F*irst, I must thank the Clear Fork Valley's local historian Martha Palm, whose newspaper articles about Cy Gatton directed my attention to his life and stories.

Thanks are also due to my friend Dan Laskin for taking a kindly interest in the stories I tell and the book I've written. He proofread the manuscript and made helpful suggestions and I am grateful.

I must thank Mercedes Sabio, top banana at WOUB-TV in Athens, Ohio, who co-produced with me the 60-minute video documentary, "Cy Gatton & the Great American Whopper." It was this program which eventually brought the names of Rick Sowash and Cy Gatton to the attention of one Jim Bissland.

It is this same Jim Bissland, editor-in-chief of the Gabriel's Horn Publishing Company, whom I must here thank most profusely. It was he who had the idea that these stories ought to be gathered into a book and it was he who labored to convince me of this. For reasons that seem silly to me now, I was hesitant to undertake such a project and I would never have done so without his persistent prodding. Once I got rolling, it was Jim who guided my hand, adjusting the word choices, polishing the sentences, organizing the stories into chapters and the chapters into a dramatic arch. We went round and round on some things— the choice of an illustrator, the color of the ink, the title of the book. His tact and knowledge and patience in dealing with my feelings on these matters eventually resulted in decisions that truly pleased all parties. The book is so much better than anything I could have done on my own that I shudder to think how it would have turned out had I been left entirely to my own devices.

Lastly, great thanks to the shade of Cy Gatton! What a debt I owe him! His stories and his personality dramatically altered the direction of my career and my life. Wherever he is, I'm sure he's

holding his own with such celebrated whopper swappers as Ananias, Baron von Munchausen and Davy Crockett. I hope to listen in on their eternal contest some day. If I can catch Cy's attention for a moment, now or later, it will be to tell him how grateful I am for the stories he told and just for being, as his neighbors down here in Ohio still say, "such a character!"

RIPSNORTING WHOPPERS!

Cyrus Miller Gatton

Introduction

A Storyteller's Story

A question people ask me often is, "How did you get started?"

To answer that question completely, I, Rick Sowash, have to tell a long story—about myself and my part of Ohio, about my grandfather and my Scoutmaster, about Cy Gatton, Mark Twain, and Johnny Appleseed. Like I say, it's a long story, but also, I think, a good one. And it even has a sort of moral at the end.

Now that I've finally written the story out, when people ask me that question, I can just hand them this book and tell them to read the introduction.

Once Upon a Time...

Nearly two centuries ago, a shabby little man by the name of John Chapman made his way into the wilderness of north central Ohio. He left in his wake a legacy of apple trees and stories. Both took root, and today every schoolchild has heard of Johnny Appleseed...an historic figure cloaked in myths.

Just 18 years after the pioneer nurseryman died, Cyrus Miller Gatton was born in the same Mohican Country that Johnny Appleseed knew so well. Both Johnny and Cy were outdoorsmen wise in the ways of nature. Both were extremely ragged in appearance, yet, in what might appear to us to be a paradox, each possessed a shrewd head for business. In yet another paradox, both "businessmen" were widely admired and even loved. And both Johnny and Cy are linked to that American tradition of humor called the tall tale.

Johnny Appleseed stuck to planting trees, letting others tell the stories, but Cy Gatton did both. For much of his life, Cy was busy raising trees and spinning tales...ripsnorting whoppers about the Heartland and its amazing soil, weather and creatures. Most of all, he told tales about himself. They were outrageous "stretchers" that would make his listeners gasp in amazement and then roar with laughter. As with Johnny, a mythology developed. Unlike most of Johnny's mythologizers, however, Cy Gatton had a sense of humor.

The real Cy Gatton (1863-1937) lived his whole life on the family farm on the Clear Fork River in north central Ohio. The area is a gently rolling countryside lying halfway between Columbus and Cleveland. It is the heart of the one state in the Union that can truthfully claim to be "the heart of it all." Here, five little rivers come together like the fingers on a hand to form the Mohican. They are the Black Fork, the Rocky Fork, the Muddy Fork, the

Cedar Fork, and Cy Gatton's beloved Clear Fork...all forks of one river, the river that has given its name to the "Mohican Country."

The great grandson of Isaac Gatton, one of the earliest settlers of Richland County, Cy grew up in the prosperous decades following the Civil War. It was a time when the richest man around was still, generally, the farmer, and storytelling was the dominant form of rural entertainment.

Like Johnny Appleseed, Cy Gatton planted trees here. But while Johnny's footloose ways carried him from Pennsylvania to Indiana, Cy stayed in one place, raising a family and a nursery business. His business, now called the Wade & Gatton Nursery, is still going strong, and it's still in the family.

We don't know when Cy started telling whoppers, but probably it was pretty early on. Most of his stories were traditional favorites, but what made them different was the way he made himself the central figure in most of them, creating a character that is Ohio's answer to Paul Bunyan, Pecos Bill, Davy Crockett, Mike Fink and John Henry (see a "A Note on Sources" at the end of this book).

Cy's first audiences were most likely his family, friends and neighbors. Then, in the 1890s, Cy developed "Gatton Rocks." This was a resort area named for the sixty-foot, pine-peppered rock formations that loom above the Clear Fork River as it passes through the Gatton farm. Cy offered vacationers family cottages for rent, swimming in the Clear Fork River and even a tennis court. People began to come down from Mansfield and Cleveland and up from Newark and Columbus. The train even made a whistle stop at Gatton Rocks.

Of course, the vacationers came for the ageless pleasures of summer: swimming and scenery. Mostly, though, they came because of Cy Gatton himself: he was such a character, a perpetrator of pranks and practical jokes. He was full of fun and bursting with stories, stories about all the amazing things that happened on that remarkable farm of his. Cy especially liked telling about the preposterous goings-on back in the woods up behind his big house. The place, known as Wildcat Hollow, had soil so fertile that he was afraid to plant anything back there until one day...but you'll encounter that story later in this book, and all in good time.

Cy's reputation as a storyteller spread. As he reached his fifties, he found himself in demand as a professional humorist, telling his stories at banquets and picnics throughout the Buckeye State. Young folks especially enjoyed Cy's stories: hundreds of older Ohioans living today recall with delight the stories they heard Cy tell at a Boy Scout or 4-H campfire.

By the mid-1930s, near the very end of his life, Cy's mastery of the tall tale brought him to national attention. Lowell Thomas, the most famous news commentator of his day (and a fellow Ohioan), heard Cy speak to a banquet audience and was captivated. Later, in a national radio broadcast, Thomas gave Cy a certificate of membership in an exclusive organization he'd founded, "The Tall Story Club of New York." The certificate itself is so delightfully worded that it's worth quoting in full:

Know all men by these presents that it is my tall privilege to give high testimony that CY GATTON, who tells them tall, with a lofty sacrifice of veracity, has proven his altitudinous devotion to The Great American Whopper, and is hereby elevated to the rank of Exalted Ananias of The Tall Story Club.

It was the high point of Cy's career, and if he had lived another ten years, Ohio might have had a nationally celebrated folk hero all its own—a kind of Mark Twain, Will Rogers and Garrison Keillor, rolled into one uniquely Buckeye character. Perhaps it's still not too late.

Cy Gatton's "Cy Gatton stories" are lovely antiques that we can still enjoy. They connect us with the past. But their fascination for modern listeners goes deeper. At the heart of each of Cy's stories there is An Unanswerable Question: why are there limits on anything? For example, what determines the maximum speed at which a plant can grow? Why can't a catfish be trained to live outside the water? Why can a dog run only so fast and no faster? Why do there have to be beginnings and endings? What is birth? What is death?

These are questions asked only by children and philosophers and perhaps an exceptional scientist. Cy Gatton didn't try to answer them. What fascinated him instead was the challenge of *posing* these questions in the guise of tall tales...stories so vividly

conceived and intensely told that they would trick people into pondering The Great Imponderables...making them think *and* laugh at the same time.

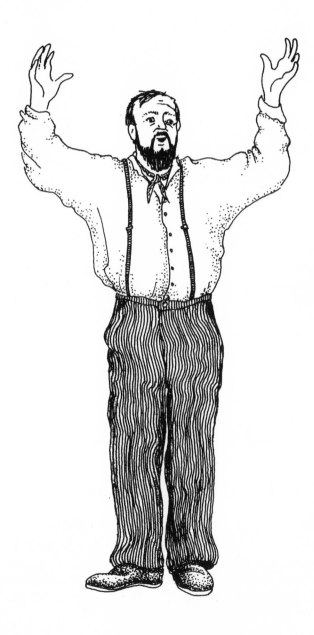

When the old storyteller died in 1937, the same thing happened to him that happened to Johnny Appleseed: the fictional Cy Gatton did not depart. Instead, he lingered on in a kind of half-life, affectionately recalled and increasingly blurred with memories of the real person who had, in effect, created him.

Nowadays, Cy Gatton the legend is very much alive and I'm proud to have played a role in nurturing and expanding it. Over a hundred times each year I stand before a group of people and tell "Cy Gatton stories." I tell them at banquets, conferences, conventions, schools, parks and libraries. Some of my listeners are adults while others are children, and some are families. All that they have in common is their fascination with the stories. Sometimes I spot a mouth hanging open and or a set of eyes popped wide with wonder. And I see these expressions not only on the faces of children but on those of adults as well. Often they look surprised, as if they had never before heard the mix of brazen falsehoods and imponderable mysteries that characterizes the best Cy Gatton stories.

These stories delighted me, too, right from the start, when I was a boy growing up in Mansfield, Ohio, and heard a few of them from my father. His parents had known Cy Gatton, too. Neither my father nor his parents were gifted storytellers, but my grandfather on my mother's side, John Hoff, was a virtuoso with an inexhaustible repertoire of all kinds of tales. Sometimes, listening to him, I could hardly keep back my tears; other times I would laugh at his grotesque sense of humor. "I haven't had so much fun," he would remark offhandedly, "since the hogs ate my little brother!"

Like many immigrants, my grandfather had embraced his new homeland of Ohio with a fervor uncommon among native-born Ohioans. Born in a German settlement in Hungary, he was the most earnest Buckeye I have ever known. He drew his sense of *who* he was from his knowledge of *where* he was. He wasn't just an American, he was a special kind of American: he was an Ohioan. He knew that Ohio is the confluence of New England and Virginia enriched to this day by a steady trickle of immigrants like himself. People came here from places near and far and they fashioned a new kind of American, a person of the Heartland, a

Midwesterner. What modern Americans call "The Midwest" is something that slowly spread northwest, west and southwest from Ohio, but here in Ohio was where it began. Before Ohio, America had no heartland; it was here that "The Midwest" was first defined.

I don't recall my grandfather ever saying a word about Cy Gatton. But he awoke in me a love of storytelling that would eventually enable me to harvest the treasures Cy Gatton had so casually tossed off and left behind.

Not long after my grandfather died, I came under the spell of another remarkable man: Frank Culp, my scoutmaster. He and Dad had been Boy Scouts together. He remembered Cy Gatton, too, and was up on his Ohio history. And, like my grandfather, he was a natural-born storyteller. From Mr. Culp I heard more Cy Gatton stories, tall tales and ghost stories and true stories of the elaborate hoaxes and practical jokes Cy set up.

I went to college, studied music and comparative literature, and married. We settled in Bellville, in the Mohican Country, and I started composing and writing in earnest. Ohio has a rich literary tradition from which I could begin, but there was no regional tradition for classical music. I puzzled over this and concluded that my preparation as a composer would have to be almost completely non-musical. Eventually, I discovered what my grandfather knew: that where we are is who we are. For creators, this is a crucial lesson. They must find out *where they are* and then plant the roots of their art firmly in that soil, expressing what they have seen and felt in living on that soil. And they must do so with a vocabulary that will be instantly accessible to ordinary local people. This is what I have tried to do with my music, my writings and the stories I tell.

Two things happened in 1977 that changed my career from a composer with "a day job" to a full-time storyteller who composes on the side. I saw Hal Holbrook's wonderfully entertaining and convincing evocation of Mark Twain. And I read an article in our local paper, the *Bellville Star & Tri-Forks Press,* about Cy Gatton and his stories. The article was lovingly written by Martha Palm, a local historian to whom I owe a great debt.

When I read that article I suddenly realized with a jolt that here, right under my nose, was a treasury of local culture reposing almost forgotten: the stories of Cy Gatton. I had more or less known those stories all my life, but now I looked at them in a new light. They were a form of truly local literature, part of the web of local patterns I was striving to absorb into my music.

I felt compelled to do something with the stories, but what? I began simply. I started telling them at family gatherings and Scout functions. I found that they had a powerful and uproarious effect, blossoming into grandiose images and unfolding with wildly improbable twists and turns. Gradually the thought came to me that I could do a theatrical re-creation of Cy Gatton just as Hal Holbrook had done with Mark Twain.

I didn't act on the idea right away: seven years went by before I finally offered Bellville my one-man show. I called it "Cy Gatton's Tales of the Clear Fork Valley." I had gathered about 90 minutes' worth of stories and mastered the knack of applying makeup to make myself look like Cy, complete with a huge mustache and a black skull cap. I had never heard Cy speak—missing him by thirteen years—but we shared a lot of the same neighbors. I lived out a dozen of the happiest years of my life in the village of Bellville, and one of the things I loved most about that place was the way older people talked there. A flat, practical, matter-of-fact way of speaking that was direct, kindly and rhythmical. When I tell Cy's stories, I try to tell them in the way I heard those older people talk, which must be a close approximation of Cy's own way of telling them.

Some of the stories I told in that first show had actually been told by Cy Gatton, but others I gathered from other storytellers, from books, and from my own adventures and memories. I didn't claim that ALL the stories were original with Cy nor with me. Like Cy, I just plucked the stories from here and there, re-assembled them, dressed them in a local setting and presented them anew, telling them as best I could.

That first show was presented in the 130-seat Bellville Opera House, the sweet little theater my wife and I had helped restore. The show sold out. Cy's descendants came out by the dozens, and scores of older people who remembered Cy came to hear him tell his stories once again. We had to run the show for a second

weekend. Again, it sold out. Later, we did another round of performances to raise money for a successful fight against a proposed hazardous waste dump near the headwaters of the Clear Fork River.

Next, I took the show to the Renaissance Theatre in nearby Mansfield, where it ran for fourteen Friday nights in a row. At home my phone began to ring. Would I come and tell those Cy Gatton stories for the local Lions Club, Boy Scouts, elementary school children, senior citizen group, Soil and Water Conservation banquet? Sure I would.

The show itself began to change. I kept picking up new stories from older people who would call or write or come up and talk to me after a performance. And it seemed to me that many of these stories might be better told in the third person. Too, I was getting tired of "being" Cy Gatton. I found I very much preferred to be myself. I did one last performance in make-up and costume at the Renaissance Theatre. We called it "Cy Gatton's Last Stand" and 600 people came out to see it.

When I dropped the make-up, I thought that the number of invitations I got to perform would decrease, but instead they have been increasing ever since. I started to charge a fee and to advertise. I hired an agent. After seven years of storytelling on the side, I launched myself as a full-time professional humorist-storyteller on January 1, 1991, and have earned most of my income that way ever since. In 1992 I wrote, produced and narrated an hour-long public television documentary on Cy Gatton and his stories, entitled "Cy Gatton & the Great American Whopper." I produced an audiotape version of the stories. And now, this book. Like John Chapman and Cy Gatton before me, I am living the life I imagined. Perhaps the personal moral of our stories was best expressed by yet another raggedy storyteller, Henry Thoreau, when he said that if we advance confidently in the direction of our dreams, we will "meet with a success unexpected in common hours."

A larger lesson my own story might have is well expressed in a question from a little-known book I dearly love, *The Harvest of a Quiet Eye,* by Odell Shepard (published by Houghton Mifflin in 1927): "What is the outlook for a land so huge that not even the traveling salesman can know it well in every part, unless every man strikes down deep roots of affection in some small and comprehensible district to which he really belongs?"

Clearly, the outlook is grim: an endless and characterless suburban wasteland of asphalt, bland housing developments, traditionless shopping malls and identical chain stores. These are locales without local history and neighborhoods with little neighborliness. They cannot be accurately described as communities. They are more like vast machines, designed only to consume, to be consumed, and to breed consumers. They are, for the most part, oblivious and even hostile to the ancient values transmitted through music and stories.

Yet, I am optimistic.

Why?

Because I have put down deep roots of affection in the little patch of the landscape to which I belong and I know the richnesses to be gained from doing so.

And because I have seen the expressions on the faces of those who have listened to these lovely, old, wise and preposterous "Cy Gatton stories."

I can tell you from an abundance of personal experience that ordinary people have a keen appetite for such richness. My audiences are not some rare, peculiarly aware, anti-materialist demographic set. They are ordinary people, typical modern-day Americans who watch TV, shop at Sprawl-Mart and have a bacon-cheeseburger now and then at the fast-food on the interstate. A great many of them live in the suburbs and probably they are more or less happy there, too.

But in spite of all that...or maybe even *because* of it...modern listeners make a deep connection with these Cy Gatton stories, as though Cy's tales are already half-familiar and hearing them anew has returned a precious, though almost-forgotten, legacy to them.

They need these stories just as much as the pioneers in John Chapman's time needed apples. It's one of the few verifiable verities: people need stories.

You should see their eyes as they listen...expressions of awe and rapture cross their faces like the shadows of clouds moving across Ohio corn fields on a summer day.

So throw a log on the fire and pour yourself a cup of steaming tea. Make sure the phone-answering machine is functioning and arrange the dog at your feet. Pull your afghan about you, my friend, and prepare to ponder....

The only thing that ear could do was swell up!

Incredible Cy Gatton

Almost anyone can tell a story and almost everyone does, sooner or later, now and again. Embarrassing moments, practical jokes, strange coincidences—we all know stories about such things. But good storytelling is an art, and an art can only have a few masters.

Cy Gatton was one of the masters. He was so masterful, in fact, that his powers of storytelling came near to landing him in a heap of trouble.

*C*y Gatton's neighbors would say, "Oh, go on now, Cy! You and your ridiculous tall tales! You expect us to *believe* this nonsense? You might fool those people from C'lumbus or Clevelun' that come down to stay at your place. People from C'lumbus and Clevelun' 'll believe most anything. But we're your *neighbors*. Don't even *try* to pull those tricks on us. Save 'em for those suckers from the city!"

Sometimes Cy pretended to be hurt by this kind of talk. He'd wrinkle his brow and say that he just couldn't understand how folks in Ohio's Clear Fork Valley could say such things about him. He'd ALWAYS made it a point to be truthful with his neighbors!

But, Cy would admit, people from Columbus and Cleveland, even people from nearby Mansfield, were different. THEY were fair game for his stories. When they came down to vacation at the little resort he ran on his farm, they *expected* to be hogwashed! It was part of the fun of being at Gatton Rocks. City people were sitting ducks. They'd lap up the most preposterous foolishness. Then, when they realized they'd been had, they'd laugh and beg for more.

Sometimes Cy thought of asking his daughter, Nell, to paint up a sign for out front of his place, to read:

GATTON ROCKS:
Legs Pulled
Mole hills enlarged
Wool gathered
Snorters ripped
Gees whizzed
Byes gollied
Curiosities piqued
Fancies tickled
Funnies cracked
Guts busted
Good fun cleaned
Goat ropings officiated

Ah, it would be a wonderful sign. And all those claims would be *true*. Cy knew he was a merciless kidder, an incurable practical joker, a teller of tall tales. But he *wasn't* a liar! Cy never told a lie in his life!

Well, that isn't *quite* true.

There had been that one time, when Cy was still a boy. He hadn't yet realized the full majesty of his powers. He had sort of tried out his mental muscles on another fellow. It was a cousin of a local boy, Jonathan Leedy, who had come out from the East to spend the summer. For once in his life, Cy did tell an actual lie— and what a lie it was. It was a great, magnificent lie, an enormous, altitudinous whopper. It would have brought a blush of pink to the cheeks of even so hardened an old liar as the Bible's Ananias.

Cy meant no harm in telling this lie. He was just testing himself, as I've said. But, as I've also said, he didn't know his own strength.

We'll never know what that lie was, because Cy wouldn't ever tell it again after he saw what happened. It was such a BIG lie, you see, that when Jonathan Leedy's cousin come to hear it, why, it made his *left ear* (Cy was standing on the fellow's *left* side when he told this lie) swell up to SEVEN TIMES its normal size!

The Creator just hadn't fashioned human ears to be able to bear such extremes. The only thing that ear could think to do when it heard such an outrageous untruth was to swell up. Oh, it was a sight to see! That ear swelled and it swelled. And it *stayed* swelled up for a preternaturally long time. After hearing such a lie, that ear could not be made to unswell...not even with the application of hourly ice packs twenty-four hours a day.

Cy was mighty sorry about it afterwards and said so to Jonathan Leedy's cousin. The fellow didn't seem to mind, though. The ear gave him no pain. Wearing his hat *was* a little hard until Cy suggested he pin up the left half of the brim. The fellow took Cy's advice and the fashion caught on. Soon all the young fellows in the Clear Fork Valley were wearing their hats pinned up on one side. Later, one of them joined the Rough Riders to fight in the Spanish-American War. Teddy Roosevelt took one look at that Buckeye's hat and right away pinned *his* brim up on the side, too. Of course the rest is history; all the other Rough Riders soon

followed suit.

Jonathan Leedy's cousin found that he could still wiggle his big ear just as good as ever. In fact, that was the trick that made him famous. For the first time in his life, he found himself a center of attention, someone worth going to see! Why? Well, because he found he could *fan* himself with it! People came from miles around to watch that fellow fan himself that way.

That left ear didn't shrink back down until the dead of the following winter. Even then it was never again quite small enough to match the fellow's other ear.

So after that, like I say, Cy didn't tell any more lies, at least not to his neighbors or to his neighbor's cousins. No, sir! He made a point of holding his powers in check. Instead, he told only *tall tales*...stories that were ALMOST true. Or, at least, they could have been. Deep down inside each one was some grain of truth...somewhere. During the summer, he would tell his tall tales to the vacationers who came to Gatton Rocks. And during the winter, he'd share them with his friends in the Clear Fork Valley Mushroom-and/or-Coon-Hunting Society.

The Mushroom-and/or-Coon-Hunting Society

We think of Cy as the constant center of attention in the Clear Fork Valley, holding forth at campfires or community meetings, or lengthening the legs of the visitors at Gatton Rocks. But actually, there were times when he was almost overshadowed by one-legged Colonel Hizey. Colonel Hizey, a veteran of a long-ago war, was a neighbor and a friend of Cy's, though secretly Cy thought him to be the most brazen, bald-faced liar he had ever met.

The Clear Fork Valley Mushroom-and/or-Coon Hunting Society was founded by Colonel Hizey upon a single principle: no one

should be allowed to join until they had shown the power of their imagination. They had to prove they could tell tall tales. Many a hopeful candidate applied. They thought that just because they could tramp about in the woods all day looking for mushrooms or prowl around all night hoping to bag a raccoon, they would be accepted into the club. Yet all but a few were turned down after members had heard them tell their stories.

Membership in that club was downright difficult to attain.

Oh, the regular members would hear out the hopefuls politely enough, giving them all the time they needed. Then Colonel Hizey would usually tell each wishful thinker that he might have talent as a politician or a reporter or a horse trader. But, he would explain, getting into the Society would require more play of fancy, more power of invention, more strength of imagination than they appeared to possess.

To this day, many seem to think that all that's required to make a good mushroom-and/or-coon hunter is the ability to tell lies easily and without blushing. That is a mistaken notion. Anybody can tell a lie. What sets the real mushroom-and/or-coon hunter apart is the ability to tell a story...a tall tale, if you will...*and make it sound absolutely true.* That requires a mastery of the circumstantial detail, the embellishing touch of probability, a general air of scrupulous truthfulness. These were the qualities needed to get into the CFVMa/oCHS, and few indeed were the men who had them.

So few, in fact, that the official membership role never exceeded half a dozen.

When Cy, old Colonel Hizey and the other members convened a meeting, they'd spend the first hour or so in what they called "hearing out the hopefuls." That meant letting those who yearned for membership show their stuff. It was mostly a lot of empty bragging, but the regular members were patient and courteous. There was but one rule observed by members of The Clear Fork Valley Mushroom-and/or-Coon Hunting Society: no story, no matter how long or shallow, should be interrupted until it was over and done with.

One "Raccoon-teur" at a time! That was the rule.

When the hopefuls had finally played themselves out, the

Colonel would remove his pipe from his mouth. Then, as he knocked out the ashes, he'd say something like, "Well, a funny thing happened to me last Tuesday but it's not much good my telling anybody about it."

"Oh? Why's that?" the hopefuls would ask.

"Because I don't expect anybody would believe me if I did," he'd reply in a matter-of-fact way and without the slightest tinge of bitterness. None of those present felt sure enough of themselves to argue with him.

Then a long silence would prevail as the Colonel became completely absorbed in the task of refilling his pipe. It seemed to be a delicate undertaking, one that required the most minute attention. He would tamp down the tobacco with the greatest care, one layer at a time, ignoring the waiting listeners. Satisfied at last, he'd light up and go on.

"No," he'd continue as he puffed, "I wouldn't believe it myself if anybody told it to me, but it's a fact, for all that and just the same."

Then would follow some really extraordinary tale that would make Cy fairly squirm just to hear it.

One time the Colonel told about the extraordinary victory he'd won over the local rat population. He said he knew of a tunnel in the ground where the rats ran through like water. They'd go in one end of the tunnel and then come out the other about ten yards away, dozens of them, maybe even hundreds. All the cows and horses around his place were afraid to go near that tunnel. The rats just got more and more numerous until the Colonel decided something had to be done about it.

The Colonel had a terrier named Apple Honey that he always said was the best coon dog around. He took Apple Honey with him one morning and they went out to where that rat tunnel was. The Colonel told how he just plugged up one end of that tunnel and quick run around to the other end, with the terrier right along side of him. Pretty soon the tunnel was just bubbling with rats, all of them scurrying about and nowhere to go. Finally the pressure and excitement of it all got to be too much for them. They begun to come popping out the open end of the tunnel, like corks out of a popgun.

The Colonel said that every time a rat popped out of the hole, Apple Honey would snap him up behind the neck and chomp down just hard enough to remove the creature from the manifold miseries of this vale of tears, once and for all. The Colonel and Apple Honey were there for the better part of an hour before the last rat come popping out.

Of course, the Colonel allowed as he hadn't made an *exact* count, but he guessed there must have been a hundred rat carcasses there at least!

Well, the whole time the Colonel was telling this rat tunnel story, Cy kept rolling his eyes and squirming, but he didn't interrupt. "One 'Raccoon-teur' at a time," he kept repeating to himself.

But when the Colonel finally wound down, Cy spoke up. Cy politely observed that Colonel Hizey was a hard act to follow. He freely admitted that he had but little of the Colonel's skill and experience. He paid his respects to the old soldier's daunting combination of natural-born ability and acquired skill.

Cy let this sink in on his audience. A long and profound silence settled over the whole room and everyone hunched forward to listen, regulars and hopefuls alike.

Then Cy told about how the Colonel's tunnel story had reminded him of the time he was out coon hunting with his muzzleloader, his lantern and his dog, Buck. He'd wandered off quite a way from home and it seemed like the night kept on getting darker and darker. After a while he saw why this was: a great, angry thunderstorm was rolling up out of the west.

Of course, he *could* have made it home if he had wanted to fight his way through the rain and the wind. Just before the storm broke, however, Cy come upon a hole in the ground. He wasn't sure, but he thought it might just have been the selfsame hole that the Colonel had later trapped those rats in. But that night, at least, there didn't appear to be any rats in the tunnel, so Cy and his dog, Buck, crept on in. They nestled down in some dry leaves to wait out the storm and Cy turned his lantern up as bright as it would go.

It really was a remarkably warm and dry little tunnel. Cy felt just as cozy as could be, what with Buck curled up there beside

him and the lantern burning bright while the storm raged outside. There's nothing makes a man feel more at-home-like than to be warm and dry while the weather is howling and pounding just a few feet away.

After a while, Cy fell sound asleep and he didn't wake up until the next morning when the sunlight come streaming through the opening of that tunnel. Then he woke up with a start and realized that the whole night had slipped away. He and Buck stretched themselves and crawled out of that tunnel. It was a beautiful day, clear the way it often is in Ohio after a storm, but Cy wasted little time taking in the scenery. He was eager to get home because he knew his wife would be worried.

Well, it wasn't 'til he'd got home that he remembered the lantern. He had left it back there in that hole in the ground!

Cy happened to be busy all during that day and the next day, too. Soon a week had gone by and he hadn't gone back to fetch his lantern. It was a long walk back to that part of the farm and Cy had to put it off.

When he finally did get back to that woods, darned if he couldn't find the hole he'd crawled into! He looked and looked, but it was no use. He thought he knew just about where it was, but wherever he looked it wasn't there and he never did find it. He figured he'd seen the last of that lantern.

A year or so later, though, he happened to go walking back there just after another great storm had come and gone. He was mighty sorry to see that the ferocious winds of that storm had blown over a grand old chestnut tree. The roots had pulled up a mighty mound of dirt and rocks when it fell, leaving a great hole in the ground where they had been. Cy climbed down into that hole and stood there, looking up at the great spread of exposed roots. All of a sudden the ground give way under him and he crashed through the floor of that hole and landed—right in that selfsame tunnel where he and Buck had slept through the storm *the year before!* There was the pile of leaves they'd slept on and— Lord a-mercy!—there was that lantern, just where he'd left it— AND IT WAS STILL BURNING!

Everybody laughed then, members and hopefuls and all. But old Colonel Hizey spoke up and said he didn't believe a word of

what Cy had said.

Then Cy said, "Tell you what I'll do, Colonel. If you'll take away ninety-five of them rats you say popped out of that rat tunnel of yours, I'll blow out the lantern!"

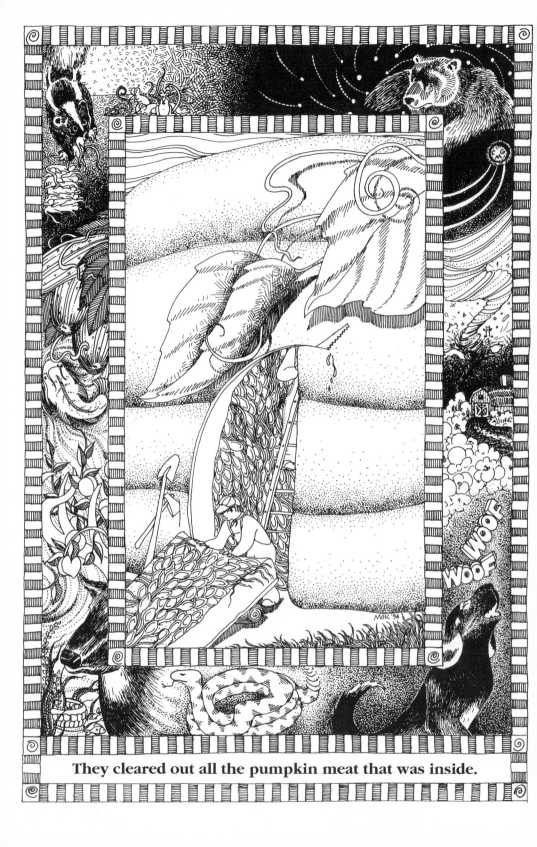

They cleared out all the pumpkin meat that was inside.

A Fer-tile Land

The most fer-tile soil on the face of the earth, the wildest whims of the weather, the curious-est cucumbers, the preposterous-est pumpkins...Who wouldn't lick their lips in anticipation of stories about such things? Well, such are the ingredients Cy Gatton tossed together in story after story.

The opening story of this chapter is full of beginnings—of glaciers and pioneers and early summer and seeds getting planted and the first big adventures of an up-and-coming Richland County boy, beardless and be-pimpled and full of pluck, as you'll see.

A Close Call in Wildcat Hollow

Now as I understand it, it's generally agreed upon amongst the scientists and experts and the people who know 'bout these things that, of all the states in the Union, Ohio has the richest soil. There's not much argument about that. But the question to be pondered is: which *county* has the richest soil in the state of Ohio?

Well, there's nothing tricky about it and it's not hard to figure. All you have to do is look at a map of Ohio to realize that there is only one county with a name that even *refers* to the quality of the soil. That's *Richland* County.

So the *real* question is, how did this one county come to have the most fer-tile soil?

It goes back to the biggest thing that ever happened in the state of Ohio, the biggest thing by far. The glaciers. That's right, the glaciers!

Ten thousand years ago a great wall of ice came down from the north pole—a great wall of ice, *five thousand* feet thick! What was it? It was the glaciers! These glaciers scooped out Lake Erie like a giant steam shovel, and then headed south, re-routing rivers, pushing and churning up all the soil in front of them and then setting it down here and there as they rumbled along.

And while the glaciers were about this mighty business, they were all the time saying to themselves things like: "Now this soil over here we're laying down once and for all in *Huron* County, and we're going to do it so as to make certain that this soil is going to *stay* in *Huron* County from *hyur on* after!

"Now take this soil over there...it's good, but it's not quite so good as that soil over here, and we got a lot to do today, so we'll put this soil off *'til tomorrow."* And that's just what they did. They lay that soil down *to Morrow* County, you see, putting it off for the farmers of the future to *till tomorrow.*

And then they said, "Now take this soil here: it's kinda gray and burnt-out and sooty looking, so we'll put it over to *Ash*land County. That only makes sense!

"And here's soil with a lot of boulders *weighin'* several hundred tons, so we'll take and put *that* soil over to *Wayne* County."

Now a lot of orphan soil deposits got all mixed around and confused. They wouldn't never have found their rightful place in the world except for the fact that the glaciers took pains to find good *homes* for 'em—over to *Holmes* County, for example.

But the best soil of all, the cream of the crop, they held back so that they could put it down to *Richland* County. And they took special pains, you need to know, to put the cream of the cream of the crop down to the *southern* end of Richland County, down in Jefferson Township, on a 700-acre plot of land. Located half-way between the present-day villages of Bellville and Butler (you can look it up on the map and visit it to this day) that 700-acre plot of land was predestined from the dawn of time to become the Gatton family farm.

And then they took extra-special particular pains, those glaciers did, to lay down the most lush and loamy, abundantly and prodigiously *fer-tile* soil—the cream of the cream of the cream of the crop—on a particular spot on that farm. It was away back in the woods, a spot that came to be known as Wildcat Hollow.

And there that soil lay for ten thousand years, getting richer and richer by the hour. Every autumn the leaves would fall from the trees and mulch that soil good, and every spring the purest water would bubble up out of the ground and slosh and rinse through that black dirt until it become just altogether unspeakably fer-tile.

And finally, right on schedule, ten thousand years after the glaciers had come and gone, along comes Isaac Gatton, the first Gatton into these parts. He was a rude and hearty pioneer, and known for his strength. But strong as he was, there was one thing he would not dare to do. *He would not plant anything out to Wildcat Hollow.*

And him a strong, brave pioneer! They say he was so strong he could take a horseshoe in his bare hands and just with the sheer strength of his hands he could take that horseshoe and tie it into a *knot*...while it was still on the horse!

But strong as he was, he would not plant anything out to Wildcat Hollow.

His arms were so strong he could grab hold of his own shirt collar and lift his entire self three feet off the ground and then set himself back down again.

But strong as he was, he would not plant anything out to Wildcat Hollow.

He got his strength by drinking rock juice. Every morning he'd go out to the garden and dig around until he found himself a big rock, and then he'd take it back to the kitchen and hold it over a little cup and squeeze it until all the juice dripped out into that cup. Then he'd throw the skin of the rock out the window and drink that cup of rock juice right on down. It was the secret of his strength.

*But strong as he was he would not plant anything out to Wildcat Hollow...*and the reason was that he was afraid to! He didn't know what might happen.

Isaac noticed early on that when he planted corn fifty yards back from Wildcat Hollow—*fifty yards back* now, mind you—the cornstalks would grow as high as a flagpole and the ears of corn would be the size of flour barrels and the silks would be as thick as ropes. He had to send his little grandson, Cy, to shinny up those cornstalks and hack those ears of corn down with a Bowie knife— it was the only way they could harvest 'em! And one ear of that corn could feed the whole family supper! And this is from cornstalks planted *fifty yards back!* No, sir! Isaac would not plant nothing out to Wildcat Hollow itself—not no way, not no how— and it was all on account of he was afraid to.

And so the years passed, and they never planted nothing out there, and that soil grew more and more fer-tile 'til it got to where you'd walk out there, and you could actually feel that soil *breathing* underneath your feet, panting in a fevered anticipation of a seed!

But, like I say, they never planted nothing out there. They were afraid to try it. And so they never did.

They never did, that is, until one never-to-be-forgotten day I

want to tell you about.

You remember I mentioned this little shaver of a grandson that Isaac had? name of Cy? The one who used to shinny up those cornstalks? Well, he was destined for great things.

Cy had gotten to the age of about fifteen or sixteen and he thought he had the world by the tail. He thought there was nothing he couldn't do. He'd brag on and on, don't you know, until his two younger brothers, Charlie and Alfred, got good and sick of hearing him.

The upshot was that one day they *dared* Cy to go out and plant something out to Wildcat Hollow. They said, "You think you're so big and strong and smart and tough? How 'bout you go out and plant somethin' out to Wildcat Hollow, now how 'bout that?"

Cy thought to himself, "Humph! Nothin' to it! Piece-a-cake! What's the big deal about plantin' anything? You take a seed and stick it in the ground—there ain't nothin' to that!"

So he allowed as he would make the attempt.

He went out to the barn and rummaged around, and the first thing he found was a sack of cucumber seeds. He grabbed a handful of those seeds, stuffed them in his pocket and set off walking out to Wildcat Hollow.

You got to realize that it was a beautiful June day—the sky was washed blue, the birds were singing, the leaves were flapping in the breeze like a billion little green flags—and here he was a-walking along, a young fool with a pocketful of cucumber seeds and...an appointment with destiny!

Well, he hadn't thought much about it. He got out there to Wildcat Hollow and reached his hand into his pocket and pulled out some of those seeds. And he was just getting ready to plant them when he noticed that something was wrong.

What was it?

He looked around him—everything *looked* all right.

And then it come over him what it was.

It was...the *silence*.

The birds had stopped singing; the wind had died down. An unnatural hush had settled over the whole forest. *Mother Nature was a-holding her breath, waiting to see what would happen.* For the first time, the most fer-tile spot in Richland County, the most fer-tile spot in the state of Ohio, the most fer-tile spot—who knows?—maybe the most fer-tile spot on the whole of God's Green Earth was finally going to be planted.

That silence pressed in on Cy from all sides. He looked around in desperation. Every little hole in the ground and every little hole in the trees had a pair of eyes peeking out at him—groundhogs and raccoons and squirrels, don't you know, waiting and watching to see what would happen.

Ten thousand years in the making and now, at last, the moment had come—the moment for the planting of *THE MOST FER-TILE SPOT!*

Cy was frightened. I don't think he'd mind me telling you. Later he admitted it himself. He said he was frightened. That silence was a-pushing in on him from all sides and thick as molasses, and it got to be more than he could bear.

He decided to call the whole thing off. He put those seeds back in his pocket and started headin' back to the barn. But then he remembered his younger brothers and how they had dared him to do this thing and how he had let on there'd be nothing to it. This recollection gave him cause to pause.

Now if you ever had younger brothers, you know what a turmoil he was going through. If you're the oldest and your younger brothers dare you to do something, it's not to be taken lightly. You got your pride to keep up. Bein's you're the oldest, you feel you got to prove yourself worthy, to say nothing of setting an example.

So he swallowed hard to keep his courage up, and he went back over to that spot. And with a trembling hand he reached down into his pocket and took out—not the whole handful, no sir! he wasn't such a fool as that!—he took out just one little itty-bitty cucumber seed.

And what *is* a seed after all? Nothing more than a sort of a little pill made of something like cardboard...and yet what a mighty lot of power there is all bound up tight in a seed.

Well, Cy knelt down there, and the moment had come!

He took and made a little hole in that soil, about two inches deep, and then he put the seed down in there and patted it over good.

He stood up and started heading back to the barn...but he had not gotten more than about five steps...when...he...heard...

an *EXPLOSION* behind him!

He looked around, and here was cucumber vines a-growing up out of the ground like a great, green fountain, a-wrapping round the trees and growing off into the woods every which direction!

He took off a-runnin' like a shot—and he was pretty fast in those days, too—but he wasn't fast enough. Here come one of these cucumber vines a-snaking along the ground after him through the woods, and it wrapped around his ankle and, by golly! it tripped him—bang!—and down he went.

Before he could get up, before he could even get up on his elbows, why, cucumber vines were growing up into his ears and down into his socks. They were even getting into his underpants! And one of them, a green cucumber vine, come a-growing up around his neck and started to choke him! He couldn't get his breath! Tighter and tighter it got!

He tried wrasslin' with it, tried breaking the stranglehold it had on him, but it was no use. He thought if he could just get to his pocketknife he could cut himself loose! So he tried to get his hand into his pocket to get to his pocketknife to cut himself loose, but he could not get his hand into his pocket! No, he could not get his hand into his pocket, on account of there was already a full-grown cucumber in his pocket! All his pockets was stuffed full of cucumbers! His shirt was full of cucumbers! His pants was full of cucumbers! His socks was full of cucumbers!

Well, it would have been the end of him. And there wouldn't have been any more Cy Gatton stories...and this would have been a mighty skinny book!...except for the fact that just then, in the nick of time, when he needed it most, along come one of them strange, freakish and unusual things that followed Cy all his long life, wherever he went and whatever he did.

Along come...*a June frost!*

Doesn't happen very often, I'll admit. But you heard right—a June frost!

Ice crystals come dropping out of the sky! Sleet, hail, snow and freezing rain! Icicles come a-slobbering down from all the little twiggy branches on the trees!

Say, that frost hit that cucumber vine right square between the eyes and knocked the ever-lovin' aspirations out of it...that cucumber vine just withered away right on the spot...and Cy Gatton's life was saved!

More Adventures in Wildcat Hollow

*I*t took Cy a whole year to get his courage worked up before he could bring himself to try planting something out to Wildcat Hollow again. But you know how it is: you get a year older, you get a year wiser. So when that year had gone by, Cy was a sight smarter than what he had been. This time, when he went out to Wildcat Hollow to plant, he didn't bring along nothing that grows quite so fast as a cucumber vine.

This time he brought along a *pumpkin* seed.

And *this* time, he knew what to expect! *This* time he didn't go kneeling down on the ground to dig no hole. No, sir! *This* time, when he got out there to Wildcat Hollow, he held that pumpkin seed up as high off'n the ground as he could reach, and then he took and dug a hole in that fer-tile soil *with his heel*. Then he got himself all poised and ready to run, and after aiming that seed real careful right above that hole, why, he dropped it, and at the same moment he took off running as fast as he could.

Well, he got out of the way in time. And he come back the next day with his two brothers, each of them pushing a wheelbarrow full of tools—saws and shovels and axes. They cut a hole in one side of that pumpkin that had grown there overnight, and then they went around and cut a hole in the other side. They cleared out all the pumpkin meat that was inside, and do you know? They were able to use that pumpkin shell that whole summer long...FOR A BARN!

Cy was careful 'bout that spot, though. He wouldn't just go out and plant any old thing out there to Wildcat Hollow. And as he got older, he became more cautious, the way most folks do.

The years slipped away, and he hadn't planted nothing out to Wildcat Hollow for the longest time. He hadn't even thought about the place much until one day in early spring he happened to notice a curious look in his son's eyes. It was a look he thought he could recognize.

"Earl!" he said to the boy. "Earl, you have the look of a young fella that's just dyin' for the taste of real corn on the cob."

And the boy said, "Pa, you read my thoughts! Right now I'd give anything for a bite of real corn on the cob."

Cy knew this longing feeling well—many a time he'd felt it himself. He always held it up as one of the crimes of creation that real Ohio corn on the cob can only be had for a few weeks out of each long year. He was about to offer what little philosophical comfort he could to ease the boy's sufferings, telling him how he'd just have to make the best of it and wait 'til July—when he happened to think of that fer-tile soil out to Wildcat Hollow.

He snapped his fingers and said, "Earl, you want corn on the cob for supper tonight? You're goin' to have it!" And he led the boy to the barn where he kept some seed corn. He picked out a kernel of that seed corn, all plump and golden, and he put it in his pocket, and the two of them set out to Wildcat Hollow, father and son.

Now, you know, corn grows awful slow, specially when compared alongside of the vining plants like cucumbers and pumpkins, so Cy wasn't too worried about any danger. He just knelt down and pushed that kernel of seed corn right into that black loamy soil, which was more luscious and fer-tile than ever. Then he stood up and him and Earl passed the time o'day while they was waiting to see what would happen.

Now I don't want to exaggerate. It might have been five minutes went by; then again, it might have been six or seven; but whatever it was, here pretty soon comes a-pushing up out of the earth a pretty little slender green sprout, like a little finger pointing up out of the ground and growing in plain sight of their very eyes.

Cy laughed and said, "Now then, Earl, you keep a close watch on that little corn stalk and let it grow to about fourteen feet or so, and then you shinny up and pull down some ears of corn and bring 'em back to the house—and we'll have 'em for supper." And, having instructed his son, Cy went back to the barnyard to see about the chores.

Well, here half an hour later, all of a sudden Cy hears somebody yelling off in the distance, yelling out: "Pa! Hey, Pa! Pa!" And it sounds like Earl! So Cy cranes his neck around looking over toward Wildcat Hollow, and he hears this yelling again.

It sounded like Earl all right, but if it was Earl that was doing the yelling, then the yelling sounds should have been coming from over to the direction of Wildcat Hollow...but they weren't a-coming from over to the direction of Wildcat Hollow, they were a-coming *straight down out of the sky above!*

So then Cy looked up, and there's Earl, clinging for dear life to the biggest corn stalk you ever did see, looming up out from Wildcat Hollow and growing higher and higher into the sky with each passing moment.

Cy yells out, "Earl! Why don't you climb down from there?" But Earl yells back and he says that he can't do it—because as fast as he tries to climb down, why that cornstalk is growing *up* even faster! For every ten feet he climbs down, he finds himself eleven feet higher up!

Cy says to himself, "I got to save my boy!" and he grabs his cross-cut bucksaw and runs out to Wildcat Hollow to the spot where they had planted that kernel of seed corn. There he finds this great green cornstalk about as big around as a full-growed oak tree, and it's rising up out of the ground lickety-split. So Cy pushed his saw into it, giving it one good stroke, but before he could even pull that saw back toward him, why, here it had already growed up out of his reach!

So then Cy runs back to the barn and grabs his axe and runs back out to Wildcat Hollow. He didn't hesitate. He reared back and give that cornstalk a mighty *whack!* But the trouble was, that cornstalk was growing up out of the ground so fast that he couldn't hit it twiced in the same spot!

Then it come over him that there was nothing to be done but wait 'til that cornstalk stopped growing of its own accord.

Well, for the next couple of weeks, Earl had all of the corn on the cob he wanted up there amongst the clouds. 'Course Cy knew the boy'd get good and sick of corn on the cob pretty quick—specially bein's how he had no way of cooking the ears away up there in the sky and no butter or salt to put on 'em in any case.

But you know, it shows how necessity really is what they say: the mother of invention. To help his boy, Cy invented one of his most famous gizmos, a sort of a cross between a slingshot and a shotgun, and he used that whatcha-ma-jigger to shoot dried peas and biscuits up to the boy so's he wouldn't starve to death!

A week later—I don't want to exaggerate; it might have been ten days—one of those terrible Mohican Country thunderstorms come a-blowing up and knocked that great cornstalk right over flat. Cy feared his son would be killed for certain, falling from such a height. But here the next day, there was a knock at the door. Cy opened it up and, by golly, it was Earl! He was a little green around the gills, but none the worse for wear.

Cy was mighty glad to see the boy, but he couldn't grasp how he had survived such a fall.

"There weren't nothin' to it, Pa," the boy explained. "By the time the storm come up, that cornstalk growed so tall that when it come down it landed me in Lake Erie, just off Sandusky. All I had to do was swim ashore and hitch a ride home."

"Well, I'll be," said Cy.

That was all he could think to say.

He couldn't make no forward progress.

The Amazing
Weather

*Good storytellers work hard. They want their
words and the pauses between them to be just so.
And they hope they'll be blessed with listeners
who'll give them the right amounts of silence and
laughter, things they cannot control.*

*Farmers work hard, too, hoping for the right
amounts of sun and rain, things THEY cannot
control.*

*When the things we want come in the right
amounts, we can all give thanks. And when they
don't...well, we can always tell more stories.*

Hot Weather in the Heartland

Y ou can well imagine that Cy watched the weather pretty close during that time, what with Earl bein' up in the clouds and all. Cy would lay awake at night and wonder how the boy was making out up there. He knew that Earl had nothing more to keep him dry than an umbrella made out of the corn leaves.

But Cy was an Ohioan and so, of course, he was *always* watching the weather. It's part of the free entertainment that comes with living in Ohio. Then, too, Cy was a farmer, and like any farmer, he was always hoping for the right amount of rain and the right amount of sun. And like all farmers, he thought if he just watched the weather close enough he might be able to get a grip on it and make it do *what* he wanted it to do and *when* he wanted it to do it.

Sometimes, too, he wondered if there was a mysterious connection between his own powers of imagination and the extremes of weather there at Gatton Rocks. But then again, maybe it was just typical Ohio weather. People in other parts of the country don't know what-all weather can be. People to the south of Ohio don't know what a cold winter is and people to the north never know the true heat of summer. People over in Pennsylvania don't know what a wind is because the hills of Ohio sap away the better part of a good breeze before it ever crosses the state line. And people in Indiana don't grasp the really amazing difference between the weather at the top of a hill and the weather down in the ravines on either side of it.

Ohio has the *best* kind of weather—but it also has all the other kinds as well. And, as they say, if you don't like the weather in Ohio, just wait a few hours and it'll change.

Cy watched the weather come and go all his life but there were a couple of amazing seasons that stuck in his mind and he liked to tell about them.

He liked to tell about the Summer of the Terrible Heat when it got so hot he had to mix in cracked ice with his chicken feed. In the terrible heat, it was the only way he could figure to keep his chickens from laying hard-boiled eggs!

The sun beat down mercilessly, day after day, and the corn in the fields got yellower and yellower until there wasn't hardly any green to be seen. The heat got worse and worse until it didn't even let up at night. It just kept on getting hotter and hotter, even after sundown. Each night before he went to bed, Cy had to throw a bucket of ice water over the thermometer he had fixed outside his kitchen window to keep it from spouting its red juice out the top.

Then one night something amazing and all-but-unheard-of occurred. Some people had been watching for it. Others said it was impossible.

But that night it got so hot that it finally happened. People woke up in the middle of that night and they heard the noise of it and they knew right away that it had happened at last.

All of the corn out in the fields had begun...TO POP!

Well, it popped and it popped. You never heard such a sound! Billions and trillions and gazillions of kernels of corn all poppin' away out there in the night.

Toward dawn the last kernels had popped themselves out, though you know how popcorn is...just when you think it's really done popping, along comes another pop...and another...and then just one more. And then it's really done. Except for one last pop. Then just one more.

There was no *crack* of dawn that morning. Instead, there was the *pop* of dawn!

But the popping finally stopped, more or less, and people looked out their windows to see a sight that had never before been seen. The whole valley lay six foot deep in popcorn!

Then, to make matters worse, the wind kicked up and blew great drifts of popcorn across the roads. They had to get out the snowplows to clear the highways.

Cy was especially curious to see how the animals would take this flood of popcorn. The chickens liked it just fine and they helped out considerable, eating their way back forth to clear a path between the house and the barn. The dog liked it OK and would eat his share, so long as Cy spread melted butter and a good sprinkle of salt across it.

But Cy had an old mule that couldn't be convinced that it wasn't snow...he took one look at all that popcorn and just quietly lay down and froze to death.

Then come...

The Winter of the Terrible Cold

*C*y kept a close watch on the thermometer outside the kitchen window, as day after day the temperature dropped. There didn't appear to be enough red stuff inside that thermometer to fill a pimple.

And then it started to get REALLY cold.

Cy was standing out in the barnyard when the first cold snap struck. He was standing there, noticing the effects of the cold. When he drew air in through his nostrils, they crackled out loud. The end of his nose and his earlobes were tingling with the cold and his fingertips were turning a pale shade of blue. The ice that was forming in his mustache had got to be a regular weight on his upper lip so that he couldn't say his P's or his B's without sounding like he was drunk.

He sucked in one last draft of that cold air, filling up his lungs with it and letting it slowly back out. Then he figured it was time to head back into the house where it was warm. "Petter pee gettin' pack to duh house," he said to himself in a mumbly sort of a way.

But when he went to take a step toward the house, why, here he found that he couldn't move!

Oh, he could move his head around all right and his arms were free enough. He could even lift his feet up off the ground. But somehow, try as he might, he couldn't make no forward

progress.

He looked around him to try to see what was going on...and then he saw where the problem was...he had been standing too close to the barn and his shadow had *frozen* onto the wall of the barn!

He yelled out for his wife, Etta Pearl, to bring out a kettle of boiling water, and quick! "Etta Burl!" he called, speaking as best he could. "Pring out some poilin' wadder, quick, peefore I vreeze tuh deff!"

So she came a-running and poured that water right down onto the shadow, holding the kettle's spout right up against the shadow of the hat on Cy's head. The water run down the whole length of that shadow and, though some of it froze in place there on the barn wall, it loosened up the shadow enough for Cy to tear loose. It made a regular ripping noise, it did. And for several weeks after that Cy noticed holes in his shadow that corresponded exactly to some gray patches that were still stuck onto the wall of the barn.

Well, after that the weather took a turn for the worse and it began to get REALLY, REALLY cold!

The coal furnace in Cy's basement couldn't hardly keep up a defense against the armies of cold air currents that attacked and invaded the house. Cy kept the furnace fired up good and he kept fires going in the fireplaces, but there wasn't a room in the house where you couldn't see your breath coming out of your own nose in great, gray clouds of steam. And when night came on, it got even colder yet.

Cy and Etta Pearl got the whole family together in one bed and threw over top of themselves every blanket, quilt, coverlet and comforter they had in the house. "Fear Not, Thy Comforter Cometh," said Cy, quoting the old hymn. They all burrowed together under there, cozy-like, and, except for the density of the population, they had to own that they felt fairly comfortable.

After a while they fell asleep.

Then, a little after midnight, Cy woke up with a troubling thought: Buck! The old farm dog, Buck! He was an outdoors dog and they never let him in the house. But when Cy thought about poor old Buck outside in that terrible cold, his heart went out to the dog. He got up, pulled on his boots and his coat and his hat and stepped out onto the front porch. The cold just about knocked him over, but let the cold do what it might, he knew he had to get Buck inside.

He looked over to where Buck's doghouse was and there he saw old Buck, already making his way toward the front porch. The dog had heard Cy open the front door and he wasn't waiting for an invitation to come inside. He appeared to be all right, but he was moving mighty slow and meanwhile the cold was assailing Cy from all sides.

So Cy thought he'd yell out, "Come on, Buck!" to encourage the dog to hurry up a bit. But when he went to yell out those three words, why, each one of those words, when they shot out from under his mustache, froze solid into an ice cube before they could even make themselves heard! And where Cy had naturally expected three *words* to come out of his mouth, here three little *ice cubes* popped out instead and landed at his feet with a plink, plank, plunk.

He tried again, but it was no good. As soon as the words hit the air, they froze solid and dropped tinkling to his feet!

So Cy had to make do with waving his arms, gesturing for Buck to come. And meanwhile Buck was doing his best, slowly making his way across the snow-covered yard to the porch.

Buck wanted to let Cy know that he was coming as fast as could. So he tried to let out a reassuring series of barks—but instead of barks coming out that dog's mouth, why out come two or three ice cubes, regular bark-shaped ice cubes! The dog tried again, but it was no use. His barks would get a good running start from deep down inside his throat, but when they hit that cold air, why, they would freeze solid before they could make themselves heard.

But Buck didn't give up. He kept coming closer to the porch and trying his best to bark as he came, leaving a trail of ice cubes across the hardened surface of the snow.

Finally Buck made it to the porch and Cy got him inside quick and rubbed him down. Then he went back upstairs and the dog followed him. The dog jumped in under the covers with the rest of the family and soon they were all asleep.

But, as it turned out, those few minutes out in the yard were

the worst of the cold. And as the family slept, things started changing outside. Warm currents of air come up the valleys from Cincinnati, laden with the scent of orange blossoms and pineapples. It was a regular thaw setting in. The icicles started dripping and the snow drifts receded from the banks of the streams.

And as the family slept on, it kept getting warmer and warmer outside. When the first hint of daylight come, Cy was laying in bed, his family and his dog all tangled up around him. His eyes was closed but he was laying there awake, letting his mind wander the way you do when you're still half asleep.

Suddenly he heard a somehow familiar voice out on the front porch yell out "Come on, Buck!"

He and Buck both sat bolt upright in bed. Again came the voice, "Come on, Buck!"

And then he recognized the voice. It was his own. He had left those ice cubes laying on the front porch, each of them with a word froze inside and when the thaw come, why the ice cubes had melted enough to set the words free into the air!

And then the barking started. It was Buck's barks, each one popping out of those bark-shaped ice cubes Buck had left in a trail behind him as he had come across the yard.

It was the only time in his life that Cy was woken up by the sound of his own voice yelling. And Cy was pretty sure, too, that it was the only time in Buck's life when *he* was woken up by the sound of his own barks!

The Buck, the Bear and the Tornado

*H*ot summers, cold winters, drought and snow, Cy saw them all at their wildest extremes. But he always said that when it came to weather there was nothing— nothing!—that could equal the fearsome ferocity or ruthless rambunctiousness of an Ohio tornado.

At the start of the day on which Cy had his closest brush with a tornado, tornadoes were the furthest thing from his mind. He wasn't thinking about tornadoes; he was thinking about big game.

It was the occasion of Cy's biennial hunting trip down to Scioto County. Much as he loved the woods and streams of the Mohican Country, Cy allowed as how he sometimes got tired of huntin' the rabbits and squirrels and little squaw deers that were to be found near to home. He longed to hunt the big game that flourishes down in the southernmost tip of Ohio. What's more, for a long time his wife, Etta Pearl, had been wanting a hat rack. So he concluded to get a big buck deer and save the antlers for a rack, as that would be cheaper and also ornamental.

Well, after he got his corn husked that fall he took out an old bear gun that had belonged to his Grandpa Isaac—that gun shot a bullet as large as a hickory nut!—and he took out his store of his own hand-made bullets. Cy always molded his own bullets, taking care to put his private mark on each one of them.

When he got to the hunting ground away down in Scioto County, the locals warned him to keep an eye peeled for a big black bear that had killed several hunters. This bear would swipe a hunter on the back of the head, coldcocking him, after sneaking up from behind.

When Cy heard these warnings, he just smiled and went on.

Before long, he spied a big buck with the largest antlers he had ever seen. There were enough points on those horns to hold all the hats at the next Gatton family reunion, so he decided to get that buck at all cost.

But the buck saw Cy first and started away through the brush. Cy followed in hot pursuit and, unrelenting, stalked that animal for hours, circling around and around through the hills.

As the afternoon wore away the wind began to blow, and though the ever-rising rush of air seemed ominous and menacing to Cy, it actually ended up saving his life.

The weather showed all the signs of a tornado brewing: the weird brown clouds scudding across the sky, the unearthly howl of the wind, the hail stones as big as a baby's fist. Cy ignored these things, determined not to be distracted as he tracked that deer.

Finally he had that buck in his sights again, but the buck looked right at him with an air of lofty indifference. And the buck paid no more attention to the worsening weather than Cy did.

The buck looked Cy dead in the eye and Cy stared right back

at him. Then Cy could see that buck's shoulders shaking and shivering. Cy thought at first that the buck might be scared. Then he thought maybe the buck was cold. But finally he realized that that buck was a-quiver with nothing less than suppressed giggles. That's right, *giggles!* The buck was laughin' at Cy outright, as much as to say, "Shoot me if you dare!"

Well, Cy had never had such a curious encounter with a beast of the woods and he almost hesitated to shoot. By now the wind was blowing so hard he had to straddle a boulder with both legs so as to keep from flying away. The sky had taken on a deathly, greenish look and everything all around was glowing with an eerie light.

The combination of the elements pounding on his body and the deer mocking his pride nearly undid Cy, truth be told. He doubtless would have turned back altogether right then if he had not recollected his wife's pressing need for a hat rack. Without another thought, he took aim on a spot right between that deer's quizzical eyes and squeezed the trigger!

But just then the wind boiled over and rediscovered itself in the form of a full-fledged tornado.

Right behind him, Cy heard an awful crash followed by a bellowing groan!

What was it? Trees falling? boulders ripping loose? streams re-routing themselves? He didn't look back to see. Nothing could have swerved his eye from that deer. The deer stared at Cy a moment more and then turned and went scamperin' away unhurt.

By now the wind had nearly jammed Cy to a jelly against the rocks and he let go of his gun so's he could cling to that boulder with all fours.

It took all the strength Cy could muster just to crank his head around, but he was determined to see what had made that great roaring crash and groan he'd heard behind him.

Well, when he looked around, here he come to find a huge black bear lying there not five feet behind him, stone dead and with a clean bullet hole the size of a hickory nut right between his eyes.

Then it was that Cy realized what had set the buck to giggling. That buck had been watching that bear a-stalkin' up behind Cy

all the time that Cy had been a-stalkin' up on the buck!

"Well, but who shot the bear?" you may ask.

Let Cy tell it in his own words.

"Who shot the bear? Why, that's just what I'm a-comin' to. The fact is, the tornado that was blowing when I fired my gun stopped the bullet flat! It blew it back over my head and struck the bear between the eyes just as he was about to coldcock me.

"How do I know it happened in this way? Hoo-hah! Because I found that out when I skinned him! Yes, sir! Deep down in the old fellow's brain I found my bullet, marked "C.M.G.," which stands for Cyrus Miller Gatton, of course, and that's the name that stands for me and none other, make no mistake!"

The Return of the Big Buck Deer

*C*y figured he'd never set eyes on that big buck deer again, but he figured wrong. Two years later he was once again hunting down in Scioto County. It was October and the weather was just grand. The leaves were so vivid and multi-colored and the sky was such a deep shade of blue that Cy found it was almost a relief to shut his eyes from time to time. Perhaps it was because of this that he hadn't had much luck.

Oh, he'd nailed a couple of wild turkeys, a half dozen rabbits, and a score of squirrels. Still, this was a far cry from his usual good luck.

It was getting on toward twilight and he was just about to write it off as a bad day when he heard an uncommon commotion in the bushes. He stood stock still and he listened and looked...and just then out from behind the bushes stepped the biggest buck deer he'd ever seen! It was the same deer that had giggled at him once before but he had grown so much that Cy could hardly recognize him. All the same, Cy could tell that was him, all right.

He was standing in a clearing not fifty yards off.

Cy went to charge up his muzzleloader but—curse his bad luck!—he found he was clean out of ammunition. He made a quick search through his coat pockets but the only thing he found was an old dried-out peach pit. Well, he thought, that was a whole lot better than nothing, so he stuffed into the gun barrel a double charge of black powder and then jammed the peach pit down on top of it.

Then he cocked his rifle and drew a careful bead on that deer. There was no wind to reckon with this time. Everything was perfect. Hardly daring to breathe, he squeezed the trigger and—BANG!—smoke rolled and branches fell to the ground all around. When the air was clear again, Cy looked and there was that big buck, still standing there, giggling sarcastically. He looked right at Cy, as if to say, "Is that the best you can do, old man?" and then he sort of shrugged his shoulders and walked off, as proud as you please.

Of course, there was nothing to do after *that* humiliation but call it a day and head on home, which is just what Cy did.

Two more years passed and not a day went by but what Cy didn't think of that magnificent buck. And when eight seasons had slipped by, Cy found himself out hunting once again away down in Scioto County and in the same part of the woods where he had encountered that deer before. And long about twilight he came upon that same clearing where he had seen the deer both times before. He looked up and there, sure enough, was the same old great big buck deer.

There was no doubt in his mind but that it was the same deer—on account of what that deer had in place of *antlers!* Where before he had had a regular fifty point hat rack, now instead he had a fine young peach sapling a-growing right out from between his eyes!

Well, of course, Cy couldn't bring himself to shoot such a curiosity as that, so he let his third chance to bag that deer pass right on by.

In the years that followed, deer hunters down in Scioto County began to notice a strange thing. They'd go out with their dogs and follow deer tracks through the woods down there in the

southernmost tip of Ohio. And when the dogs would come upon a spot where the deer had left a ripe little pile of fresh-laid dingleberries, why they'd roll in it, of course, the way dogs will do, no matter how much we yell at them for doing it.* There was nothing in the least odd or unusual about that. The funny part was this: instead of *stinking* afterwards, those dogs would give off the unmistakable scent of peach preserves!

Some thought it was because the deer had taken to nibbling the bark off peach trees.

When Cy heard that theory, he just smiled.

---

* Cy is credited with having discovered the reason behind this previously unexplained behavior of dogs. "They do it to disguise their scent," Cy explained. "Say a dog rolls hisself in the remains of a dead fish, gettin' it all over his shoulders good, the way they like to do. Why, then, don't you see? Later on when he's chasin' a couple of deer through the woods, one of those deer'll stop and sniff the air and then turn to the other one and say, 'You know, I could *swear* I caught the scent of a *dog* followin' us through the woods!' The other deer'll sniff the air and think it over for a minute before he says, 'Naw! That ain't no *dog* followin' us through the woods—it's a *dead fish* that's after us!' Then the first one'll sniff again and say, 'I guess you're about right. It's a dead fish sure enough!'"

Maybe pickles do like lemmings do: mass suicide!

Pickle Bridge

A life is a bridge that crosses the turbulent chasm separating birth and death, a beginning and an end. A story is a much smaller bridge between an opening "Once there was..." and a closing "...so that was how it all came out!"

Stories like Cy's, old stories, make another kind of bridge as well, a bridge between our nation's past and present. Cy Gatton's particular life spanned two dark shores of American history: the Civil War and the Great Depression and, in turn, his stories bridge the gap between those times and ours. Bridges, bridges, bridges! Indeed, in one of the stories from Cy's time, the hero itself is a bridge!

Head out of Bellville on Durbin Road and you come to a sudden curve in the road, right at the edge of town. You better not keep going straight, because if you do you'll end up in the river. But time was when you'd have gone *across* the river instead of *into* it, because there used to be a bridge there. And what a bridge it was!

There hasn't been a bridge there for many years, but the location is popular with the locals as a good place to fish. And everybody still calls the spot "Pickle Bridge."

"Oh, yeah," you'll hear people say in Bellville. "Caught me a nice mess o' blue gill last evening out to Pickle Bridge."

The funny thing is that, when there really was a bridge there, nobody called it Pickle Bridge. It had a far more glorious name.

Oddly enough, it didn't get encumbered with that pickle-y name (or maybe I should say it didn't get "cucumbered") until after it was destroyed.

It's the strange story of that bridge's two names that I want to tell.

Pickle Bridge was already famous before anyone called it that. It became famous in the first place for surviving a major catastrophe that was freakish enough in its way. But, strange to tell, the circumstance that gave it that immortal name was the freakish calamity—and what a calamitous freak it was!—that destroyed it.

It was a covered bridge, the last one in Jefferson Township. Everybody loves a covered bridge, of course, and no one is quite sure why most have been torn down. But even if this bridge *hadn't* been a covered bridge, people would still have loved it. That's because it was a regular hero among bridges during the Great Flood of 1913.

The Great Flood of 1913 was the worst flood Ohio ever saw. It just about wiped out Dayton and the lower reaches of Cincinnati and it was no small affair in Richland County, either. The snow was still laying thick and heavy on the ground in March of that

year. Then a torrential rain began and didn't stop until it melted all that snow and swelled up the rivers higher than anyone could remember.

The flood swept away all the bridges along the entire 23-mile length of the Clear Fork River, all the way from Ontario almost to Loudonville. It swept away all the bridges, I say...*except this one!*

Though the raging torrent gnawed hard and tugged mightily, that bridge clung to its foundations. It was the *only* way people had to get back and forth between Mt. Vernon and Mansfield during that terrible time! Any number of lives were saved simply because that bridge stayed in its place; it never abandoned its post. Doctors rushing out to deliver babies or comfort the sick could get across the river. Goods and foodstuffs needed by the flood victims could pass back and forth. And just by staying there, that bridge became a symbol of hope to people.

After the waters had gone down, people didn't forget the bridge that stood firm. They were so grateful that they put a sign on it proclaiming it "The Hero of the Clear Fork." The sign told how, of all the bridges that spanned the Clear Fork, only this one had withstood the Great Flood of 1913.

Old postcards show the sign very clearly. It was a point of local pride for many years...right up to the time of a strange calamity. That calamity brought the proud old bridge down at last and changed its name from "The Hero of the Clear Fork" to its present-day moniker..."Pickle Bridge."

Cy Gatton was among the first to come upon the signs of this calamity. Like so many other insights and adventures Cy had, it came about because he was partial to the practice of simply going out to walk around and observe things. It's amazing what all a person can notice if they pick up this habit.

Now, to understand what happened that day, you need to know that the Gatton place is *downstream* a couple of miles from Pickle Bridge. I'll just tell you that right out flat and ask you to bear it in mind.

Cy was walking down by the river one summer day when he saw something floating by that give him pause.

It was a pickle.

"That's funny," he thought, but he just figured that some

picnickers had dropped it. Or maybe a fisherman had been trying to eat lunch with one hand and bait a hook with the other and had let this fine, plump pickle fall in the river.

But then he saw *another* pickle come a-bobbing along not far behind the first one. So he figured that maybe some kids had thought it might be funny to put two pickles in the water to have a race. Or maybe try to throw stones at 'em and sink 'em. Cy knew he could have flicked a flat "skipper rock" across the river and sliced those pickles, neat and clean. But neither of these two pickles weren't even *nicked!*

Then he spotted a *third* pickle, and a *fourth* and a *fifth!* So he guessed that maybe a whole gang of kids must have been having a pickle fight in the river somewheres upstream. He'd never heard of anybody having a pickle fight before, but he couldn't think of any other explanation that held water. Those kids' moms sure would be mad when they found out the pickles they'd put up had been wasted that way!

He stepped out onto a rock and shaded his eyes to get a better look—and darned if there weren't a dozen more pickles a-following right behind! Those first few merely had been the advance guard sent on ahead to shout back to those behind some clear directions as to how they could best proceed so as to skirt the shoals. And behind those dozen bobbed a hundred more, and way back, bringing up the rear—Cy could hardly believe his eyes!—there came a mighty swarm of pickles, thousands of them, flocks and hordes and schools and packs of pickles, a regular Armada of Gherkins, all floating down the river and glittering merrily in the summer sunlight as they progressed majestically on their way.

Well, Cy had heard and seen some amazing things in his time, but nothing to top this! It was like something out of one of his own stories! What on earth could be the explanation?

Was it a mass exodus of kosher dills led by some bearded old Moses of a cucumber who had finally prevailed upon whatever stubborn pharaoh had been keeping them in bondage, to "let my pickles go!"?

Had somebody left the back door open in the Bellville Pickle Factory so that all the cucumbers escaped before they could be slaughtered and soaked in brine? The main problem with *that* theory was that there was no such thing as a Bellville Pickle Factory, never was and most likely never will be.

And anyway, they weren't cucumbers, they were *pickles,* as Cy found out when he waded out and grabbed one and chewed a bite off the end of it. It was pickled, all right. No doubt of that.

Were pickles maybe a migratory species, like ducks and geese?

Or did they swim upstream to spawn like salmon? But if that was so, then why were all these pickles coming *down*stream?

Were pickles like lemmings, maybe? Cy had read about those

creatures. Maybe pickles do like lemmings do: once every couple of generations they all set out together to commit mass suicide by flinging themselves into the first big body of water they come onto. But these pickles didn't appear to be suicidally depressed. In fact, they looked to be in the pink of good health, or should I say, "the green"?

Maybe after a long and one-sided association with our troubled species, pickles had just discovered they'd had enough of the human race. Perhaps they had decided to cut loose from people altogether and set out to have adventures on their own. It was a sad commentary on the sons of Adam, Cy thought. Abandoned even by the lowly pickle.

That left dogs as our only remaining non-human friends, unless you counted horses and cats. Horses? Well, yes. But cats? Phew! Cy never could understand how cats had gained their footing as domestic pets in the first place. They live at our expense and what do they give us in return? Yet his place was always swarming with cats. Cy Gatton had cats the way some people have mice. Cats! Best not to dwell on the matter. At least we don't *eat* cats, Cy thought. Not generally, anyway.

Cucumbers must have gotten fed up with being stuffed into quart jars with grape leaves, garlic and dill, only to be drowned in salt water. They had had all they were going to take, come to the end of the line, reached their limit, thank you very much. They were heading out for greener pastures and the Clear Fork was the route they were taking. It was an explanation Cy could well understand and, truth be told, he was content with it.

The actual truth of the matter turned out to be far less colorful than any of Cy's inspired guesses.

A truck loaded with pickle barrels had made the turn onto "The Hero of the Clear Fork" at too great a speed. All the pickle barrels had slid to one side with such force as to tilt the truck over. It had crashed into the downstream wall of the old covered bridge and the beams underneath had given way. Then the truck fell over sideways into the river and the barrels burst open, spilling their contents. Now the pickles were free to pursue an Impossible Dream, bound downstream in hopes of making their way to who knows where? Some kind of Pickle Paradise, the details of which

could not be imagined, not even by the great Cy Gatton himself.

Of course, a lot of those pickles never even made it to Butler, let alone to Pickle Paradise. Cy and some other folks downstream caught a good number of them, but a lot more got lodged in along the edge of the river. For many years afterward you could go down there and see the pickle trees that grew up thirty and forty feet high from the pickles that had gotten stuck down near Gatton Rocks.

Sad to say, "The Hero of the Clear Fork" was never rebuilt after it was destroyed by the careening pickle truck. A lot of people today have forgotten that there actually *was* a bridge there once, and a celebrated one at that.

But if anybody says they been fishing over to "Pickle Bridge," most people in Bellville will know right away where they mean.

He started sewing that dog back up.

The Wonderful Pets

Cy lived in a slower time than our own. Just one lifetime away it was, when everyone owned a horse and only the rich could afford to own a car. Today, of course, everyone owns a car and only the rich can afford to own a horse!

People then had time for stories and they had time for plenty of pets. Cy put the two together to give us stories about pets...and very peculiar pets they were.

Cy and the Skunk

*C*y used to say, "The animals are Earth's children and we are close of kin to all of them, born of the same wild old mother, fed at her breast like them, and soon to fall asleep just as they do, in her strong old arms."

Cy loved animals and everything to do with animals. He loved to wander in the woods to study their ways. He loved to stare down into ponds and streams and rivers. He loved to hunt and fish. No wonder so many of his stories are about animals.

It wasn't only out in the woods that Cy met up with animals. At the Gatton home, too, there were always animals around. Cy kept cows and horses and goats and chickens, of course, but he also kept all sorts of pets, both common and unusual. Dogs and cats, to be sure, but also raccoons, squirrels, groundhogs and even skunks!

A skunk'll make a good pet, Cy used to maintain, if you take care to snip off its odor bags while it's still a pup.

This one particular pet skunk Cy had was the best mouser he had ever seen. It cleaned the entire mouse population out of the house and barn and outbuildings, putting all the cats to shame and out of business.

From eating all those mice, that skunk got so fat that just watching it waddle around the barnyard was hilarious. It would roll back and forth as it walked, burbling along like a fat old rich lady all dressed up in her best black-and-white fur coat.

The mouse population in and around the Gatton home got so small that Cy's pet skunk had to range out further and further from the house and barnyard in search of mice. And that nearly turned out to be its undoing.

One time the skunk had wandered away over back behind Wildcat Hollow where several families of foxes had been giving the neighborhood fits, dragging off the chickens and scaring the sheep. Cy had put out a couple of traps and darned if this pet

skunk didn't go wandering right into one of them. Snap! went the trap and, cruel though it is to tell, the steel jaws of that vicious trap just clipped that skunk's right front leg clean off.

Somehow the skunk made it back home. Cy was sorely distressed to see his fat little pet come limping up onto the front porch. With a tear in his eye, Cy cradled that skunk in his arms and brought him into the kitchen. He bandaged up the stump of that skunk's leg as best he could and he fed him supper with an eyedropper, squirting a nourishing mixture of warm milk and brown sugar right down his throat.

It was touch and go with that skunk. Cy thought around toward midnight that he was going to lose him. The skunk's eyes glazed over and he got stiff as a board from the shock he'd been through. Cy sat up all night with him, keeping a cool cloth on his forehead and a warm blanket around his bottom.

Happily, Cy's efforts were rewarded. When the dawn come, that skunk sat up pretty as you please and all but smiled at its master. The next day he was even better and by the end of the week he was able to hobble around the house on his three legs.

Cy was relieved and thought he wouldn't have to worry about him any more. But that's just where he was wrong.

After another week or two went by, Cy began to notice that that skunk was not as fat as it used to be. In fact, it was getting skinnier and skinnier. After another month or so it was down to the size of a normal skunk, having lost more than thirty pounds, as best Cy could estimate.

What was the trouble? That's what Cy wanted to know. He pondered on it and studied that skunk from a distance for many an hour before it finally come to him. That poor skunk couldn't catch mice any more! He was just too slow on his three legs and the mice were outrunning him! Soon, he was so skinny that there wasn't hardly anything left of him and he looked like a slack-jawed, black-and-white bag of bones.

Meanwhile, the mouse population was booming. Cy realized that if something wasn't done soon, that skunk was going to pass on to its final reward. And the Gatton place was going to be overrun with rodents.

Cy bore down on the problem. He put his mind to it and he

strained his brain. After a day or two he come up an idea. He took some old harness and sliced it up just so, notching it with a row of little holes up the middle and fastening a tiny buckle or two onto it, just so. Then he looked in the woods until he found just the right sort of stick. He took out his pocketknife and carved that stick 'til it was just the way he wanted it, rounding out a sort of a little bowl in one end. Then he used some brass tacks to connect the harness he'd altered right onto that little stick in several places.

Finally, when all was ready, Cy got hold of that skunk and slipped the harness on over its head, taking care to fit the rounded-out end of the stick right over the stump of that skunk's missing leg. Cy had rigged up for that skunk a regular wooden leg, the first animal prosthesis ever to be seen in Richland County!

The skunk quickly got the hang of it and it wasn't long before he began to fatten up again.

Cy always got a big kick out of watching that skunk catch mice after that. That skunk would hide behind a corner and when a mouse ran by, he'd jump out and grab ahold of it with his good leg and then whack him over the head with his wooden leg.

Cy figured it was a merciful way of relieving a lot of mice of their miserable existences, and it wasn't long before that skunk had grown fatter than ever!

Cy's Pet Wildcat

You would think that the cats around the Gatton place would have been humiliated to confront such a phenomenon: a skunk with a wooden leg being a better mouser than any of the cats. But Cy's cats didn't care much about catching mice. They ate other things instead, as you are about to find out.

City folks who stayed for a week or two at Gatton Rocks, Cy's

summer resort on the Clear Fork River, always showed a lively curiosity about Cy's pets and about the neighborhood fauna in general. They were especially interested in the question of the existence of wildcats in Wildcat Hollow. They used to say to him, "Now, tell us the truth, Cy! Are there really wildcats out to Wildcat Hollow?"

You can't get a straight answer out of a fellow like Cy Gatton. When people from Mansfield, Columbus or Cleveland would ask him a question like that, he would look them straight in the eye and say, "Wildcats out to Wildcat Hollow? Huh! Does a one-legged duck swim in circles? Figure it out for yourself! Uh-*course* there's wildcats out to Wildcat Hollow! Why do you think we—"

And then he would tell them how he had found a kitten of a wildcat out there one time, and how he had brought her home and kept her for a pet. She was an ordinary little kitten—a wildcat, but ordinary in every other way. Give her a bowl of milk, she'd lap it up; give her a ball of yarn, she'd jump on it, play with it, bat it around the way a kitten'll do.

But after about a week or so they noticed that there wasn't hardly anything left of that ball of yarn they give her, and they began to wonder just what that kitten could be doing with that yarn. So they peeked around corners when she didn't know they were looking, and here they come to find that kitten was *eatin'* that yarn down! That's right, nibbling it on down, suckin' it down like spaghetti!—slurp!—forty, fifty, sixty yards a week!

Now they knew it couldn't be good for her so they tried to tell her not to do it. But you can't tell a wildcat what to do—they're not gonna to listen to you! So when that first ball of yarn was gone, well, they give her another one, and she started right in on *that* one!

It didn't seem to bother her, so after a while they didn't think much about it. They'd go in to Bellville on Saturdays to get the grocery things, and they'd stop and get a ball of yarn for the cat.

They just took it for granted.

They paid it no mind.

They give no thought.

Paid no attention to it...until two years later, when that kitten come to have her first litter of her own little baby kittens...and do

you know?

Every one of those little kittens she had was born...
WITH SWEATERS ON!

Cy & The World's Fastest Huntin' Dog

Cy's pet wildcat was extraordinary, no doubt about it. But of all the animals he kept for pets during his long and colorful life, the most celebrated by far was Cy Gatton's huntin' dog.

This dog was so fast...sometimes when it got to running full speed, it would get to the tree before the coon did!

This dog was so fast...sometimes when it got to running full speed, it would take three people just to *see* him!

One to say, "Here he comes!"

Another to say, "Here he is!"

And a third to say, "There he went!"

Sometimes, when he got running *really* fast, they had to have a fourth person on hand to say, "What was that?"

But the thing was, none of his neighbors would believe Cy about this dog.

They'd say, "Oh you go on, now, with your tall tales. Save 'em for folks from C'lumbus or Clevelun'! *They'll* believe anything!"

But he'd say, "No, I'm tellin' you, it's true. I have the fastest dog—"

"Oh, pshaw, Cy Gatton! You and your dog!"

Well, finally the day come when Cy'd had just about enough of his neighbors' skeptical ways of thinking. So he said, "All right. You think you have a *faster* huntin' dog than what I've got? We'll just have ourselves a race! You be at my farm this coming Saturday afternoon with any dogs you think might be faster than mine and we'll just see once and for all who has the fastest dog."

So that Saturday afternoon come around. You should have seen all those dogs lined up, their masters holding them back by the leash.

Right from the moment they showed up, you could tell already which dog was going to win that race. Cy's dog was the only one getting warmed up! There he was, *doing push-ups*.

What they did was, they got a little red fox, swift and sly, and they let it loose. They let that fox run about a hundred yards in front of those dogs and then they cut 'em loose and those dogs took off after that fox.

Right from the start, Cy's dog was out in front of the rest of 'em, leaving 'em a mile behind, dodging the rocks, the trees, zipping across the fields, leaping over the streams, lickety-split! Pretty quick he got to running like I told you, so fast that it took three people to *see* him.

Now the fox was fast too, but he wasn't *that* fast.

He kept looking over his shoulder and noticing this one dog a-gaining on him. It was Cy Gatton's dog, coming on strong!

Then the fox begun to realize that *swift* wasn't going to cut it. He was going to have to start being *sly*.

But what was he going to do? Here he was, a fox, running across a bare, empty, open field. There weren't no holes in the ground, there weren't no hollow trees or fallen logs. How was that fox going to be sly?

Well, it just so happened that Fate or Destiny or Providence or whatever you want to call it put in the path of that fox on that historic day an opportunity...in the form of...a mowing scythe. A long-handled farm tool with a razor-sharp blade, three feet long, a-laying there in the grass.

That same morning, you see, Cy had been out in that same field, a-mowing with that mowing scythe and, forgetting all about the race, he had left that scythe laying there in the field, with its razor-sharp blade sticking three feet up straight toward the heavens.

Now along come that fox and he sees that mowing scythe and he thinks to himself, "Here's my chance!"

He runs right alongside the handle of that scythe, narrowly missing that razor-sharp blade.

Then he runs up to the top of the hill and he stops.

Picture him with me now, a red fox, sitting up on top of that green hill, with the blue skies of Richland County behind him and a smug little smile on his lips as he watches the·world's fastest hunting dog bear down on that mowing scythe, a-following his scent!

Now you know a dog don't see so good. A dog, he don't see as good as you and me. A dog sees the world in a kind of a dim and doggy way. A dog sees mostly with his *nose,* you might say, following the scent of whatever he's after.

So along comes this dog, full speed. Imagine the force behind that dog, covering forty or fifty feet with every second that went by.

That dog's not thinking about no mowing scythe. He's not thinking about no razor-sharp blade, three feet long, sticking straight up toward the heavens. No, sir! He's thinking about that fox! Following its scent right across that field.

He looks up in the distance and here with what dim sight he does have, he sees a red blur up on top of that hill and he knows it's the fox. He thinks, "I'm going to have him! I'm going to have that fox between my jaws! Oh, another four, five seconds, I'm going to have him!"

All the time, drawing nearer and nearer to that razor-sharp blade, laying there in the grass—unbeknownst to him, but beknownst to us—sticking three feet up straight towards the heavens.

Readers, fasten your seat belts. Take a deep breath and put both hands on your stomach. I hate to tell you what happened next but I've come this far and it's too late to stop.

Well, to make a long story...interminable!...the razor-sharp blade of that mowing scythe caught that dog *right between the eyes!* And it *sliced him in half,* right on down through the middle, from the tip of his nose right on through to the tip of his tail.

Guzzzzzzilk!

AND BOTH HALVES OF THAT DOG WAS STILL RUNNING!

Only they was running around, crazy-like, in circles, and Cy could see he was going to lose the race.

So Cy run up to where that dog was and he grabbed one half

of him under one arm and he grabbed the other half of him under his other arm. Then he took and slapped the two halves of that dog back together. He whipped out a needle he had along with him and some thread, and he started sewing that dog back up. He commenced to sew under the chin and he'd got a few good stitches in place when all of sudden he heard *barking* behind him. It was the rest of the dogs and only a hundred yards behind!

Say, that needle flew in his fingers. He sewed as fast and hard as a man can sew, working his way down the belly and up and around the tail, all the time a-watching them dogs coming up from behind. They were only fifty yards away!

He sewed across to where the collar would have been. The dogs were only twenty-five yards behind!

He only had about ten more stitches to go!

uh-ten, nine, eight, seven, six—

the dogs was almost on him—

uh-five, four, three, two—

and just as the dogs come up, he tied the final knot!

Then he looked back to examine his work, don't you know, and why...why...why...what do you think?

Cy had been paying so much attention to those dogs coming up from behind that he hadn't been watching what he was doing. He had sewn that dog back together with TWO OF HIS LEGS GOING *DOWN* AND TWO OF 'EM GOING *UP!*

But do you know that dog was EVEN FASTER after that?

Why sure! He'd run along on two of those legs and when he got tired, why, he'd just flip over and make a fresh start on the other two!

(Now, Reader, you ought to stand warned that there was a lot of stories told about that dog later on that were not true.

No, you never would-a heard Cy claim that dog could bark out of both ends after that. People just made that up.)

That catfish grabbed on to the hem of her long dress.

Cy and the Catfish

*Some things—like cucumbers and catfish, for
instance—just seem to be funny, all by themselves.
Who can say why? You've already heard stories
Cy liked to tell about cucumbers, both pickled
and un-. Here are some of his catfish stories.*

*It wasn't only furry animals that Cy kept as pets.
He had a couple of finny ones, too, over the years
and the most remarkable of these was his
celebrated pet catfish.*

*C*y spent a lot of time down along the Clear Fork River, standing on a swinging bridge that used to be down there, near Gatton Rocks. The swinging bridge is long since gone. Like "The Hero of the Clear Fork," it came down and nobody put it back up. But there are many pictures of it, pictures of old-fashioned-looking little girls and boys posing on it or in front of it, alongside the river's edge.

Like I say, Cy loved to stand on that bridge, gazing down into the clear waters that passed beneath and thinking about nothing in particular. It was a favorite pastime of his, and on particularly pleasant days he'd often bring along a sandwich and an apple and spend a good part of the afternoon doing that. He didn't need a fishing pole to justify his indolence. He was perfectly happy to stand there on that bridge and let be.

He was out in the middle of that swinging bridge one bright June day when, looking into the passing current of the Clear Fork, he happened to notice a catfish.

Now there was certainly nothing unusual about this, in and of itself. Catfish have always been plentiful in the Clear Fork, though they are not as plentiful now as they were in Cy's time. And they weren't as plentiful then as they had been in the early days when Cy's Grandpa Isaac had first carved that farm out of the wilderness.

Many a time Cy had heard his Grandpa Isaac tell how they had started to pasture the cows on one side of the river, with the plan of herding them over to the other for milking, and then herding them back again to pasture, and this twice a day. It seemed a good enough plan, but they had to give it up on account of the catfish in the river.

You see, when Isaac went to round up those cows after they had grazed for half a day, why, of course their udders would be filled up and bulging 'til they was just about to burst, and with the sweetest milk anybody ever tasted. But when Isaac herded 'em across the river for milking on the other side, why, here he found

their udders were all slack and empty as a born loser's marble bag!

So, he'd herd them back over again, not having taken so much as a pint of milk and when another half-day had passed, sure enough, their udders would be filled to bursting again—until they got out on the other side of the river! And then, once again, there'd be no milk to be had for love nor money.

He couldn't figure what the trouble was until he noticed the catfish swarming through the water round his knees as he was herding the cows across the river. Then it come to him: in the time it took to herd those cows from one side of the river to the other, those catfish were sucking all the udders dry!

'Course, when Cy come to learn of this, he had the idea right away of attaching string and hooks onto each of the four nipples of one of the family cows. Then he'd lead the cow into the river and back out again—and every time he'd come back with four plump catfish to show for his trouble.

Anyway, like I say, it was no surprise to Cy that he should see a catfish as he stood there on the swinging bridge.

But what *was* surprising was that this particular catfish should *wink* at him the way he did, sly and funny-like. Cy couldn't help but smile when he saw that wink and he knew right then that he and that catfish was going to be friends.

He happened to have along with him a sandwich he'd made that morning and tucked in his coat pocket. Now he pulled that sandwich out and he tugged a little piece of bread off it and rolled it into a ball. Then he took and flung that little breadball out into the river and—say!—that catfish come up out of the water about a foot into the air and caught that breadball between his jaws before ever it hit the water!

This was something like! Cy come down off the bridge and got alongside the river on the water's edge and rolled up another breadball. He could see that catfish out there in the water, watching his every move. Cy balanced that breadball on his thumb and flicked it with his forefinger so that it flew out over the river about fifteen feet and, once again, up come that catfish and snapped it right out of the air.

Then Cy began to experiment. He tossed a series of breadballs to that catfish, in such a way that each one hit the water a little

closer to shore—and every time, that catfish caught those breadballs in mid-air.

Then Cy made yet another breadball, but this time he didn't throw it. This time he set it down, floating, just about a foot out into the river, where the water was slow and shallow. The catfish took notice of this and seemed to study the situation. Then Cy saw that catfish go clear over to the far side of the river and he wondered what would happen next. A few seconds more and Cy sees a strange mound of bubbling, burbling water coming up from the far side of the river. That catfish was winding up for the pitch! That mound of water churned up more and more violent-like and then—zoom!—it started across the river at a terrific speed. Every fin that catfish had was twirling like a windmill in a tornado! He came a-sliding and a-slooshing right through that shallow water, plowing through the mud, which seemed to slow him down, until he was almost to that breadball. He had to kind of shinny on his front fins the last couple of inches, but darned if that catfish didn't finally manage to grab hold of that breadball and make off with it back into the river!

When Cy saw this he let out a "Hallelujah!" and he resolved to come back to that spot with a loaf of bread every day from then on.

And that's just what he did. Every day he'd come back and that catfish would be there waiting for him, winking at him and smacking his lips in anticipation of his daily portion of breadballs. Well, of course, Cy worked with him, real careful-like, coaxing him closer and closer to shore.

After about a week of this training, Cy felt the time had come to try an experiment. He made sure the catfish was watching him and then, in full view of the catfish's hungry gaze, rolled up a particularly large breadball and spit on it to make it sweet. Then he laid that breadball right on the very line that separates the edge of the water from the beach.

The catfish eyed the situation as if to say, "So, you want to challenge me, do you?" Then he went over to the far side of the river and did fully five minutes of his mightiest churning and burbling before he come a-zipping across the water, fairly flying right on top the surface of the river until—bingo!—he snapped up

that breadball.

Well, in another week or ten days Cy had begun to coax that rascally catfish out of the river altogether—first he brought him out two inches, then four, then six and each time that catfish stayed out a little longer. And by the middle of July, Cy had that catfish out on the beach there alongside the river for half an hour at a time, teaching him tricks!

He started with the usual tricks you'd teach an animal—roll over, play dead, shake hands, say your prayers. Then, one day when Cy had his harmonica along, he discovered that that catfish was musical. Cy would play "Turkey in the Straw" and he could hardly keep from laughing to see the way that catfish would get up on its hind fins and polka back and forth and from side to side. Cy brought along an old barrel hoop from the barn on one occasion and in no time at all he had that catfish leaping up two feet in the air from a standing position to pass through that barrel hoop!

Then Cy got to working on what he thought would be the greatest trick of all: he tried to teach that catfish to leap up from the ground right into his coat pocket. He held a big, juicy breadball right close to the pocket and he spread his legs and bent both his knees to give the catfish every advantage. He called out to him and coaxed him, "Come on, boy! I know you can do it! Up you go, boy! Here's a mighty tasty breadball a-waitin' for you! Up! Up!"

Oh, the catfish would leap and strain and try just as hard as he could, but somehow he couldn't quite make it up to the pocket. Cy was so engrossed in the process of training the catfish to master this trick that he paid no attention to what was going on around him until all of a sudden he felt a big cold raindrop land on the back of his neck. He looked up and here was one of these summer thunderstorms Ohio's so famous for, blowing up quick out of the west.

His first thought was of his horses. They were fenced in near the barn, but the barn door was closed. Without so much as a backward glance, Cy ran to the barn, but he didn't make it in time. Time he got there, the horses was both spooked and soaked and he had his hands full getting them inside the barn, soothed and

blanketed down.

Then Cy went into the kitchen, himself all soaked to the skin and spattered with mud and manure. He was taking off his things to hang them out to dry on the backs of the kitchen chairs when he noticed something in his coat pocket. What the—?

It was the *catfish!*

He had managed to leap into that pocket just as Cy had looked up to see the thunderstorm. Cy had never noticed him there during all the time he was fussing with the horses.

Cy looked outside. It was getting dark now and the rain was coming down harder than ever. He sure didn't want to go back out into that rain and clear down to the river if he didn't absolutely have to. So Cy got out that catfish and took a good look at him. He had never seen a healthier looking catfish. And for his part, the catfish just winked at Cy in his usual comical way as if to say, "Everything's goin' to be just fine!"

So Cy set him down in the corner of the kitchen and made him as comfortable as he could, figuring he'd take the catfish back to the river first thing in the morning. He put a blanket there for him and a big bowl of breadballs and another big bowl full of sweet milk.

Then Cy opened the mail and read the paper and sat by the fire for a while, smoking his pipe, and finally it got to be nine o'clock and time to go upstairs to bed. He went out to the kitchen to check on the catfish once more, and found him sound asleep and rolled up in his blanket. Half the milk and breadballs were gone. Then Cy went up to bed.

Well, about three o'clock in the morning, the catfish got to feeling lonely. He was used to having his brothers and sisters nearby, you see, all together in a school of catfish back in the river. He was enjoying his adventure on shore, but, like I say, he was lonely. He squirmed out of that blanket he'd wrapped himself in and made his way across the kitchen floor and out in to the hall to the bottom of the stairs. One at a time he climbed those stairs and when he got to the top he had to sniff around at a couple of doors until he made sure which one was Cy's. He pushed that door open and stole across the braided rug to the nearest leg of Cy's bed. It took some doing, but finally that catfish managed to

climb up the bedpost. He slipped under the covers and explored and adjusted until he got his head up on the pillow, right along Cy's head. Then he pulled Cy's great walrus mustache over his shoulder, just like you or I would do with a blanket to make ourselves feel cozy..and he drifted off to sleep.

All night Cy kept dreaming he was down at the river's edge and when he woke up the next morning he knew why: the first thing he smelled was catfish! He had to laugh at the way that catfish had just moved in and made himself to home, laying there with its fins folded behind its head, eyes closed and a little smile on its lips!

A Catfish Companion

Well, after that, of course, Cy just kept that catfish on for a pet. And he was no longer just "a catfish"—he had gotten to be The Catfish and a regular feature in the Gatton family life. When Etta Pearl would come down in the morning to make the bacon and biscuits for breakfast, that Catfish had a funny way of grabbing on to the hem of her long dress and riding around the kitchen, swinging and swaying to right and left as she went about her business.

Winter rolled by, March came and went just like it always does, in like a lion and out like a lamb, and soon blessed June had come upon the Mohican Country once more.

Cy and that Catfish went everywhere together; they were inseparable. The Catfish would ride along in Cy's pocket, no matter where he was going or what he was doing. Oh, they were the best of friends.

The two of them were so much alike, for one thing. Always fooling about and playing tricks. That Catfish would sometimes play dead in such earnest that Cy would get really alarmed. It

would lay on the ground with its fins sticking out stiff, its tongue hanging out sideways and its eyes rolled back in its head. And it wouldn't move a muscle for the longest time, not even to breathe. At first, Cy fell for the stunt and would cradle that Catfish in his arms, cooing over it and on the edge of tears. But just when a catch would come into Cy's throat, that Catfish would blink his eyes once or twice and then wink at Cy in the most comical, devilish way. Then Cy would stomp and swear and pretend to be angry, though really he thought it was funny, it being just the sort of trick he would play himself from time to time, falling down and clutching at his chest in public as though he was suffering a heart failure. When Cy finally did die, few would believe it, you know.

Well, like I say, it was June once more and Cy packed up a sandwich and an apple and headed down to the river to while away a couple of hours on the swinging bridge, peering into the water and letting the thoughts dance about in his head just as they pleased.

That day, as he stood there in the middle of the bridge, he thought back over his long life, nourishing himself from within with his memories....

As he stood there, one of the hairs of his mustache must have somehow corkscrewed and curlicued its way up into his nose, because all of sudden he felt that he had an overpowering and irresistible desire to sneeze.

Cy jerked his head back, sucking in air, and then he let loose. That sneeze fairly *exploded* out of him! And the sound of the sneeze was followed by the sound of something going—flop!—into the water.

The first thing Cy did was to check his false teeth, thinking they had flown out of his mouth with the force of the sneeze— but no, his false teeth were still there. So what had caused the flopping sound?

Then he felt down into his pocket and he realized that the Catfish was gone!

The Catfish had leaped out of his pocket, startled, no doubt, by the sneeze—and he had fallen into the river.

In a panic, Cy ran down off the bridge, alongside the river. Clothes and all he waded right in, struggling to get out to the

middle as fast as he could...but it was too late. Just as he got out there, the Catfish come bobbing up to the surface, belly first and its head and tail arched backwards.

With many a mournful moan, Cy took the carcass over to the shore and gently laid it on the ground. It was a pitiable sight to see. No more lively fits and starts, no more dancing to Cy's harmonica music, no more snuggling next to his mustache by night or leaping into his pockets by day. Its fins were sticking out stiff, its tongue was hanging out sideways and its eyes was rolled back in its head. Cy kept a halfways-hopeful watch for the longest time, but the catfish didn't move a muscle.

At last Cy lifted that Catfish to cradle him in his arms for the last time, cooing over it and on the edge of tears. And just when a catch come into Cy's throat, that Catfish blinked his eyes once or twice and give Cy the most comical, devilish, rascally wink of mischief you ever saw!

Then Cy stomped and swore! For once he didn't have to pretend to be angry, though really he thought it was funny, it being just the sort of trick he would play himself.

But that Catfish just looked up at him, all droll and witty like, as if to say, "Why you old fool! You ought to of knowed better'n to believe that a *catfish* could ever *drown!*"

"Great big ziggety-zags!" he said. "What next!"

The Diamond-Studded Ramrod

We often wonder if the past wasn't a lot more glorious than the boring present. But the truth is, the sun rose and set then exactly the way it does today. Good things happened and bad things happened. And even then people wondered if the past hadn't been a lot better than the present.

That is why Cy Gatton told stories about the Good Old Days, because people always think things long ago just had to have been better all around.

*C*y found lots of animals to hunt and plenty of fish to catch in the woods of Ohio, I can tell you. Still, he knew that the supply of game in his day wasn't as good as it had been in the heroic days of his Grampa Isaac.

In fact, one of Cy's most cherished possessions had come down to him from the great hunts of those old days. It was a muzzle-loading, double-barreled shotgun that had belonged to Grampa Isaac. The gun itself wasn't worth much, just a rusty old blunderbuss that Isaac had patched back together so many times you'd hardly recognize it as a gun. It was the very gun that he had used in the hunting stories Cy had heard as a boy.

Like I say, the gun wasn't worth much, but the ramrod that came with it—well, that was another matter. It was a *diamond-studded* ramrod and it was a beautiful sight to see. Cy's Grampa Isaac had fashioned it from a hickory stick and decorated it with some of the diamonds the pioneers used to find so easily in the streambeds that fed the Clear Fork River. Those diamonds were easy to find for the simple reason that they had a way of standing out all sparkly next to their drab, gray pebble neighbors.

Diamonds were everywhere in those days. Gold, too. And something else that, sometimes, could prove more valuable than any amount of gold and diamonds: namely, beanholes. You won't read a word about those treasures in the history books for the simple reason that they were closely guarded secrets. We all know what happens once the word gets out that gold's been discovered. The whole region goes downhill fast! Just look at California! No, sir! Things like diamonds and gold and beanholes were never openly discussed by the early settlers in Ohio. They were too precious to be the subject of a lot of cheap, loose talk.

So, if a pioneer such as Grampa Isaac wanted to decorate a ramrod, well then, all right. He'd poke around in a couple of streambeds until he'd picked up as many diamonds he needed.

If Grampa Isaac wanted to send back East for something he couldn't make himself, something like, say, a fine new spinet

piano for Cy's Aunt Rachel, well then, all right. He'd pick up a couple of rocks he knew about out to Wildcat Hollow and pull out just enough gold from under them to make the purchase.

And if Grampa Isaac was hungry in the woods and had wandered too far from home to get back for supper, well then, all right. He'd dig down into the soil in a couple of places he knew and open up a beanhole. A hundred gallons or more he'd find sometimes! Baked beans! Richly laden with molasses, ketchup and mustard! Right there in the ground. And *hot*, too! Like those bubbling hot springs and geysers and fumeroles you hear about out to Yellowstone, a regular *geo-thermal* phenomenon, never fully explained. Isaac would pull up just about a quart or so, no more than what he needed. He'd gather some wild onions and break them up raw on top of those beans. "Ah!" he used to say with a sigh. "Now THAT was eatin'!"

I'm sorry to say, though, the beanholes and the gold and the diamonds were all pretty much played out by Cy's time, and the game, too. Oh, there was still plenty to shoot at, and even to this day a lot of fellows in the Mohican Country still hunt 'coons and squirrels. And most of them still manage to get the single deer the law allows every November. But it's not like it once was. It's been quite a spell since anyone has come upon a beanhole that hadn't already long since been opened and gobbled up.

But in Grampa Isaac's day, there were plenty of beanholes. And diamonds. And gold. And wild game. *Usually*, that is. Grampa used to tell how, one fine autumn day, he decided to go hunting for duck or for goose or for whatever presented itself. He wasn't particular. He went down to the Clear Fork River where it has flowed past the Gatton place ever since the glaciers left. Then he waded out to a little island in the middle of the stream.

Well, he sat and he sat. He sat there for three days straight and not so much as a sparrow flew by. He couldn't believe his bad luck! But Isaac was a stubborn man and he made up his mind not to go home until he had something to show for his trouble. So he opened up a nearby beanhole and settled in to stay for as long it took.

With nothing to do out there, he'd load both barrels of that shotgun and then, after a while, he'd forget that he had loaded

them. So he'd load the shotgun again, ramming home the charges with that diamond-studded ramrod he'd made for himself. Before he knew it, he had close to a dozen charges in that gun.

Just about the time he was getting really discouraged, he heard something go *quaaaack, quaaaack, quaaaack*! He looked *up* the river and there were a thousand ducks swimming downstream right toward him. "By ziggety!" he said. "Now *this* is somethin' like!"

He was just taking a careful aim when he heard a *honnnk, honnnk, honnnk* behind him. He looked around *down* the river and there he saw a thousand *geese* swimming upstream right toward him. "Zig-zig-ziggety!" he said. "Now I don't know whether to shoot duck or goose!"

Moving around like that after sitting still for three days, he must have disturbed something. Grampa Isaac heard a buzzing sound and looked down—here was a great big old rattlesnake that had crawled up right between his legs! That snake lay there coiled up and ready to strike! "I'll be ziggety-zig-zig-zigged!" said the intrepid pioneer. "What's a fellow to do?"

Just then he heard a deep *mmggrrrrrufff, mmggrrrrrufff, mmggrrrrrufff* behind him. He looked over his shoulder and here was a grizzly bear rising right out of the bushes. "Great big ziggety-zags!" he said. "What next!"

Well, by now Isaac felt pretty blue because he thought his days on this earth were over. He figured he was gone every way in the world, come what might.

Then he looked up and there stood a big old buck deer over on the other side of the river and it was the biggest deer he'd ever seen in his life. It must have had seventy-five or eighty points on its antlers—the kind of deer hunters only dream of. Then Isaac knew what to do! "If I'm going to die, I might just as well die happy," he said. So he decided to shoot that deer.

But he'd grown so excited that he had forgotten to take the diamond-studded ramrod out of his gun. He took aim, all unbeknownst, and pulled both triggers at once.

Well, with all those charges in that gun, and the ramrod to boot, the gun just up and totally exploded!

One barrel blew up into a thousand pieces and they all flew

upstream and killed those thousand ducks!

The other barrel blew up into a thousand pieces and they all flew *downstream* and killed those thousand *geese!*

The trigger guard shot directly down into the ground and cut that snake's head clean off!

The stock flew over Isaac's shoulders and gave the grizzly bear such a blow on the sternum that it killed him outright!

And the ramrod went flying across the river and sent that deer to its reward!

Then Isaac had to get busy—and quick! As he later told the story of it to his little grandson, Cy, "The first thing I had to do was to get those ducks and geese to keep 'em all from washin' away. So I waded out there to gather 'em up, and every time I'd come out with a load of ducks and geese, why, my pants'd be all full of *fish!* The pants was loose at the top, and the lower ends, bein's they were tucked into my boots, prevented the fish from escaping! In all, I counted fourteen black bass, a seven-pound carp, a half bushel of suckers, three mud turtles and two water dogs. Fish, ducks and geese! I had a time stackin' all that stuff up!"

Finally, he'd retrieved all he could and he went over to take a look at that deer. The deer was dead all right—the diamond-studded ramrod had gone right through him. Still, Isaac was upset because the ramrod itself was nowhere to be found. He felt he'd lost his most prized possession and he was fit to be tied.

Then he noticed that he could tell where the ramrod had gone. After it had passed clean through the deer, it had drilled through the big trees that used to grow over to that side of the river, and, one by one, had split 'em all wide open.

Isaac started following the trail of split-open trees along through the woods. Pretty soon he knew he was getting close to the ramrod itself, because it had apparently grown weary of splitting trees open and had started simply drilling through them instead.

Finally, he looked up ahead and there was that diamond-studded ramrod he had fashioned for himself, sticking into a tree!

Its flight had finally been stopped by a tough old hickory...and it had no less than *nine quails* pinned right on it!

Cy knew he couldn't keep his grip much longer.

Curious Creatures of Waters and Woods

Aesop, Uncle Remus, A.A. Milne and Kenneth Grahame gave us wonderful stories about animals who speak. Their creatures don't seem like animals, but people disguised as animals.

The animals in Cy Gatton's stories don't speak. They are actual animals, even if they do unusual things. However fantastic its branches and blossoms may be, a Tall Tale must be rooted firmly in reality.

Cy and The Ducks

Most of Cy's stories don't have much in the way of what anybody would call a "moral," but this next one does. Let the moral be stated in advance so you can appreciate the wisdom of it: when you do a good deed in this world you never know but how it might come back to you in some way. Yes, sir!

There's a pond on the Gatton place, not too far from the big old farmhouse. Cy was always fond of watching the ducks that stopped by there on their way south each fall.

He'd take pains to put feed out there for them. Although he would shoot ducks elsewhere in the county, he never would take a shot at any of the ducks on his pond, he was so fond of just watching their habits.

Well, one year the cold weather come late, a lot later than usual. Every morning, Cy would get up and look out the kitchen window at the pond. He would expect the ducks to be gone, having flown on south. But every morning there they would be, flocked together and floating about on the surface of that pond, all quacking and squawking like ducks'll do.

It got to be so late in the year that Cy began to think maybe he should try to shoo them off on their journey south. But that year it didn't even turn cold until well after Christmas, not 'til the middle of January.

When the cold finally come, it come all of a sudden and the ducks were caught completely off guard.

They'd all gone to sleep the night before, floating on the surface of that pond, just as cozy and content as you please. None of them expected what was coming.

As they slept through the night, the ice quietly formed around their ankles. When they woke up the next morning, here they were: every one of them ducks was stuck in the thin sheet of ice that had formed over the surface of that pond. Oh, they flapped

their wings and strained and struggled, but it was no use. They were stuck and there wasn't a thing they could do about it.

Cy looked out at those ducks and saw them all sitting there, as they had all fall, week after week. He thought nothing about it, though. He didn't notice the thin sheet of clear ice that had covered the pond. Cy went on about his chores and all day long that sheet of ice kept getting thicker and thicker.

He heard the ducks squawking and quacking and complaining but there wasn't anything unusual about that—it's what ducks do! Oh, they might have been a little louder than usual, but Cy give it no thought.

However, the next morning when he looked out, Cy saw snow a-skittering across the pond and all the ducks, each of them right in the same places where they had been the morning before. Then Cy realized what had happened.

He went out to the pond to take a closer look to see what he might do to help. By this time the ice was a foot thick and he didn't see how he could chop them loose without doing the ducks harm.

My, but he felt sorry for those ducks. "You crazy ducks should of all been on your way south two months ago!" he said. "Now just look at you!"

But the ducks weren't looking at each other. They were bearing down on Cy and each of them with a such piteous, helpless look in its eyes that Cy could hardly bear it.

He went out to the barn and brought back a couple bucketfuls of feed and scattered it around where the ducks could get at it. They were mighty grateful. Cy could see that from the way they gulped that feed down.

So after that it got to be a regular thing Cy did along with his other chores. Every morning he take a couple of buckets of feed out to those ducks and on Sundays he'd put down little teacups full of hot chocolate for 'em as well. Those ducks sure did appreciate it! Cy was careful not to be *too* good to them, so's not to spoil them and take away their natural desire for flying south in the fall like they was supposed to.

The winter wore on and finally the spring thaw come in.

Day by day, Cy watched that pond, studying the thickness of the ice. It kept getting thinner and thinner, of course, as the weather warmed. And the ducks had been flapping their wings all winter long, to get exercise and keep in shape.

At last come a day in mid-March when the temperature climbed up into the fifties. Cy happened to be looking at those ducks at just the right moment. They all were flapping their wings, hard, and what with all that flapping, why, here the entire surface of the pond started to lift up into the air, carried by those ducks!

Cy stood there in amazement. He'd never seen or heard of anything like it.

That giant disc of thin ice floated through the sky, a perfect outline of the shape of his pond. And from underneath, Cy could see those ducks' webbed feet sticking through, hundreds of 'em.

Well, they flew about a half a mile, keeping that acre of ice perfectly level. But then a little breeze kicked up or maybe those ducks veered into a tilt on purpose—Cy was never sure which—but, anyway, when that huge disc of ice tilted like that, why, all the duck manure that had collected there over the whole winter long slid off. It fertilized Cy's whole back forty, saving him at least a couple of days of hard work, shoveling and spreading cow manure onto that field!

So, you see? When you do a good deed in this world you never know but how it might come back to you in some way that you don't even have the faintest inkling of when you're doing the good deed in the first place. Yes, sir!

Cy and the Wintry Woodpecker

*T*he ducks had learned their lesson and they never stayed that late again. But the creatures of the woods don't seem to share with each other the lessons they've learned. However smart the ducks had become, there were a few other birds that still didn't catch on.

Cy was coming home from the woods after a day of winter woodchopping. He had been working hard and he felt wonderfully good, the way you do when you've worked hard outside on a freezing-cold day.

He was crossing an empty, open field with not a tree anywhere near, when he heard the unmistakable sound of a woodpecker pecking away: pock-pock-pock-pock-pock! pock-pock-pock-pock-pock! The sound of that woodpecker was coming from near at hand and not a tree within a hundred yards, mind you!

Cy wondered what could be going on. A woodpecker had no business being in Richland County in the dead of winter. Still, here he was. For some reason he'd lingered after all his brothers and sisters had flown on south. Cy figured the woodpecker's travel schedule was his own business in any case. But why would a woodpecker be *pecking* out in the middle of an open field with no trees around?

Cy followed the sound and he soon had the answer to his question. There was the woodpecker perched on a stone in the field, pecking away with all his might. And with each peck a spark flew—sparks which were not wasted, let me tell you!

First with one foot and then with the other, that woodpecker was grabbing those sparks! As Cy watched, it finally dawned on him what that woodpecker was up to. It was obvious enough, once it struck him. That woodpecker was *warming his feet!*

Cy watched him a while longer and then said, "Fly on south, you crazy fool!"

The woodpecker looked at Cy for a moment with his head tilted, thoughtful-like. Then he suddenly stood up straight, as much as to say, "Not a bad idea!"

Then he flew up into the air and headed off over the hills toward Fredericktown. Cy felt sure he wouldn't stop flying until he had reached the Mason-Dixon Line.

Cy and the Owl

*C*y wanted to know all he could about the creatures that share the Mohican Country with humans. He was always watching them and he rarely missed a chance to study their curious ways.

Late in the afternoon of a November day, Cy was out walking in the woods when he heard the distinctive rhythmical hoot of an owl. "Who cooks for *you?*"the owl called out, just like they always do. "Who cooks for *you?*"

Cy wondered if he could stalk out the particular tree where that owl was perched. He stood still, a-listening for another call and soon it came, "Who cooks for *you?*"

He headed in the direction that call seemed to be coming from. After a few more stops and starts, he found the right tree. He peered up into its branches and there sat the very owl he'd been hearing, a big, fat, pompous-looking old fellow, peering down at him with his great, wide, frowning eyes.

The two of them looked straight into each other's eyes, the old storyteller and the emblem of wisdom, and neither of them so much as blinked.

Never ceasing to hold that owl's fierce, round eyes in his gaze, Cy took a step and the owl's eyes followed him. Cy took another step, and another, and the owl, curious to know what was going on, twisted his head around a few degrees, staring right into Cy's eyes all the while. Cy walked halfway around that tree and the owl turned its head half-way around, watching his every move.

Then Cy went *all* the way around that tree, craning his neck up and over sideways so's to never cease or interrupt in the slightest his end of the staring contest he'd gotten himself into. The owl continued to follow Cy's progress, turning his head around in a complete circle, the way owls can do.

Cy walked around the tree a *second* time, in the same direction, and the owl continued to twist his head. A *third* time

Cy went around that tree! And a *fourth* and a *fifth!* And *still* the owl kept turning and twisting his head in the same direction, and neither of them winked.

Around and around they went, the two of them, faster and faster, Cy on foot and the owl turning its head. Cy was getting dizzy and puffing for breath and his neck was getting stiff, but he never unlocked his eyes from the stare he'd fixed on that owl's eyes.

That old owl was *equally* determined not be outstared. That owl's head just turned around and around, over and over again, until finally, on the thirteenth go-round, it rolled right off his shoulders and fell to the ground at Cy's feet.

That owl had twisted its head around so often that it had finally come *unscrewed!*

Well, then Cy felt bad about this unexpected development he'd brought to pass. He hadn't meant that old owl no harm. He picked up its head and climbed up into that tree where the rest of the owl was still sitting. Of course, the rest of the owl didn't fly away. Not having his head, why, of course, he couldn't use his eyes or his ears and he could neither see nor hear Cy a-coming! So it was no trouble for Cy to put his left arm around that owl's shoulders and hold him place while he screwed the head back on, one half-turn at a time, with his right hand.

Naturally, once the head was re-attached, the owl felt a little shy of a human being that close. He flapped off into the woods to settle in another tree.

As Cy walked back home, he wondered if the owl's voice would be harmed from having his head screwed off and then back on again. But soon Cy heard that old owl again, asking the same old question: "Who cooks for *you?* Who cooks for *you?*"

Getting Even With Mosquitoes

*B*ut perhaps the owl *was* af-
fected by the experience after all. Maybe he flew off to live
somewhere else. Cy never saw him again, for one thing. But the
next summer the mosquitoes got as big and as bad out to Wildcat
Hollow as they had ever been. Cy hadn't realized until that owl
was gone how much good the owl had done by keeping the
mosquitoes under control in Wildcat Hollow.

Ordinarily, owls are more interested in eating mice and
shrews and such. They don't eat mosquitoes because they're too
small to bother with—*ordinarily!* But the mosquitoes out to
Wildcat Hollow are hardly what you'd call ordinary.

There's a lot of good things to be said for Wildcat Hollow but
the mosquitoes are not one of them. Wildcat Hollow mosquitoes
are big, mean, blood-thirsty and vengeful.

Cy would sometimes sift through the owl pellets he'd find
around the bases of the trees in Wildcat Hollow so as to retrieve
the mosquito stingers out of them. The he'd take those stingers
back home and use them in place of ten-penny nails.

The Wildcat Hollow mosquito clan pretty much wiped out the
surrounding squirrel and chipmunk populations. Ten or twelve
of those mosquitoes would swoop down on an unsuspecting
baby squirrel or chipmunk. They'd fasten hold of him and fly back
up, a-carrying him off into the woods so's to devour him at their
leisure.

This interfered with Cy's pursuit of the pleasures of squirrel
hunting and he hated to see chipmunks end that way, there being
no more lovable and fun-loving creature on God's green earth. He
figured he'd just have to put up with it, though, until that old owl
come back of it's own accord. And he *did* put up with it for a time.

But then the mosquitoes went too far. They come over to the
farm all in a mass one night and swooped down on Cy's old horse.
When Cy went out the next morning, he saw that those blood-

thirsty mosquitoes hadn't left nothing of that horse except for his bones. And when Cy got closer he saw that the biggest of those mosquitoes were *pitching* the very horseshoes that had been worn by the deceased beast to decide which one of them would get the saddle!

Well, right then Cy concluded that the time had come to take matters in hand.

From old Divelbiss, Cy's German cattle farmer neighbor, he got a couple pounds of fresh beef liver, all dark and dripping with blood. He set the whole mass of it in the back of his wagon, right out in the open where the mosquitoes could get a good whiff of it. Then he loaded onto that wagon a big old iron pot he used to make apple butter. He stuck a hammer in his belt, and, with a look of grim determination on his face that was fearful to see, Cy Gatton set out for Wildcat Hollow.

As he rode along, a great swarm of mosquitoes followed behind, sniffing at that beef liver. When Cy got right into the heart of Wildcat Hollow, he took that iron pot and set it on the ground, upside down. Then he gathered up the beef liver into his arms and slipped inside that pot.

It was close inside there, what with that fresh beef liver and all, and it was more than a little cramped, too, but Cy thought if the squirrels and chipmunks was ever to re-populate, then the mosquitoes was going to have to be dealt with. And that was to say nothing of getting revenge on the mosquitoes for what they had done to his horse. Cramped or no, Cy was bound and determined to see this project through.

He waited in there for half an hour or so, a-listening to the mosquitoes swirling around outside that pot, singing and humming and getting hungrier by the minute.

Finally, one of them made bold to land on the outside surface of that iron pot. The mosquito paused for a minute to get his bearings and to make sure he was safe. Then, feeling cocky, he commenced to drill his stinger right on through the pot, in an effort to get to that beef liver. This was exactly what Cy had been waiting for. He watched and he waited until that mosquito's stinger had come through about an inch and a half and then he took his hammer and give that stinger a careful little *whack,* bending it over sideways, so's the mosquito couldn't get loose.

Well, once the other mosquitoes saw this one mosquito sitting there drilling away with no apparent harm coming to him, why, they *all* joined in, and commenced to drill their stingers through that pot.

Cy was in there for the better part of an hour and he had his hands full, whacking those stingers over sideways just as fast as they were coming in.

And after another hour or so, here they were—every mosquito in Wildcat Hollow—all of them with their stingers bent over sideways. They covered the entire outside surface of that iron pot. And all of them flapping their wings in a vain effort to get loose.

It was then that there come about a development which Cy had not anticipated. You see, all those mosquitoes, all of them flapping their wings and with their stingers stuck in like that, why...what do you think? You've probably guessed it already. Yes, sir! That iron pot begun to RISE!

Up it went, first a foot or so into the air. Cy was still so absorbed in whacking the last of those stingers that at first he didn't grasp what was happening. Up it went a little further, that iron pot, and soon the iron handle was hanging down, swinging back and forth like a trapeze. Dropping his hammer, Cy grabbed hold of that handle with both hands, trying to retain possession of his apple butter pot. But those mosquitoes were flapping their wings so hard that the pot continued to rise. Up and up it went, and Cy found himself lifted into the air to a height of eight or ten feet!

Meanwhile a breeze had kicked up out of the west and Cy found himself drifting along at a pretty good clip, heading over Cutnaw Road in the general direction of Butler. By now he was twenty feet in the air and his fingers were getting mighty tired from keeping a grip on that handle, what with his whole weight hanging down. Cy knew he couldn't keep his grip much longer and he was afraid to get any higher. So, with regrets, he let loose and landed in a heap on the dusty road.

Of course, being free of his weight, that pot fairly flew right up into the air with a swoosh. Soon those mosquitoes had lifted it to the height of a hundred feet or so.

Cy stood up and watched them go, disappearing over the trees and heading off full speed toward Butler, Perrysville, Loudonville and other points east, and carrying off that old apple butter pot.

At last the pot had drifted out of sight, away up into the clouds over east. Cy turned with a sigh and headed back to the farm, thinking he'd seen the last of the old vessel.

But just on a chance, he placed an ad in the Loudonville paper. He described the pot, stating that if anyone happened to come upon it, they should get in touch with him. And here, by golly, a week or two later, there come a letter from a farmer over in Ashland County, saying he had found an iron pot that fit Cy's description.

Cy went over and looked up that farmer, who led him to a woodlot he had toward the back of his property. Sure enough, it was Cy's iron pot all right, caught high up in the branches of an old beech tree. And all around the base of that tree, scattered and littered on the ground, were the carcasses of several thousand of those giant mosquitoes.

After a while they must have weakened from the strain of flying with that pot and they had lowered into that tree, after which they had all slowly starved to death and dropped dead to the ground. It was a miserable way to go, but Cy figured they deserved it after what they had done to all the squirrels and chipmunks, to say nothing of his horse. In fact, when Cy reflected again on how they had been so saucy as to pitch the very horseshoes of their victim, his smile was downright broad. "Justice," was what he said.

Well, it required no small amount of trouble to get that iron pot down out of that beech tree, but Cy was determined to retrieve it. After a deal of doing, he managed to get it back home.

Of course, he couldn't use it to make apple butter anymore, bein's it was all full of holes from them mosquitoes' stingers.

But what he *did* was, he set that pot up on a tripod and sluiced fresh stream water into it using a special chute he constructed. That was how Cy come to invent the first shower bath that was ever seen in Richland County!

As usual, he was looking up....

Startling
Snakes

Of course, Cy knew that things like mosquitoes and snakes and houseflies and other creatures we call pests are really blessings. They're all part of the natural balance of things.

Whenever he could, Cy passed on his knowledge to young people. He usually mixed in a little practical wisdom along with the stories—just good simple truths about life.

"Are your stories really true?"
the little ones would sometimes ask Cy. And he would answer,
"There's a grain of truth in every story and there's a million
different kinds of truth."

When Cy would speak to young people's groups—Boy
Scouts, Girl Scouts, 4-H, what have you—he would always mix
in a simple bit of advice. Sometimes, for example, he'd say, "When
you go out walking, get in the habit of *lookin' up!*"

That was it. That was all there was to it. Just: "Look up!"

"If you go through life lookin' *down* all the time," he'd say,
"you'll find pennies, it's true. And how many of you here have
ever found a penny? Raise your hand if you have!"

Most everybody would raise their hand.

"You were lookin' *down* then, weren't you? Nobody ever
found a penny by lookin' up. No! You want to find pennies? Look
down." He'd pause for a minute to let this sink in and then he'd
add, "But if you want to find a far richer treasure than any amount
of pennies, then you got to get yourself in the habit of *lookin' up!*"

And then he would spin out for his listeners a list of all the
marvelous things a person can harvest by going through life
looking up. "The flocks of geese flyin' overhead, the majestic
processions of the clouds on a summer day, the shiftin' of the
seasons, the stars splangin' across the sky, or just the moon! Say,
you'll never get tired of lookin' at the moon. These are but a few
of the thousand things, big and little, that you notice when you
look up!"

And he practiced what he preached.

He was out one day, walking along over toward Wildcat
Hollow, with no companion other than his favorite walking stick.
As usual, he was looking up. He was noticing things, all sorts of
things, as he ambled along out there, looking up...when all of a
sudden he heard a *rattle* in the grass!

Now this is a sound which, even if you've never heard it
before, you hear it the first time and you're going to know right

away what it is. You've guessed it already, I'm sure.

For once in his life Cy looked *down* and pretty quick, too.

There, coiled up right at his feet, coiled up, I say, and ready to spring, its hooded eyes sparkling with a malevolent gleam and its waggly tongue a-bobbing back and forth, was *a king-sized Wildcat Hollow RATTLESNAKE.*

Oh, I hate to tell you what happened next. I hope you're not squeamish. Before Cy could take a step backwards or even try to jump out of harm's way, why, that snake made a *lunge* at him. It sunk its poisonous, venomous fangs *two inches deep—*

TWO INCHES DEEP—

guzzzzzittttt!

right into his *walking stick!*

That's right, the snake had *bitten* the walking stick.

Well, Cy knew what was going to happen. Any doctor, any veterinarian, any boy or girl who's growing up in the country could tell you just what was going to happen next and just what to expect.

Cy knew what to expect. That was why he took off running back to the barnyard as fast as he could go. But he had not gotten even half-way back before that walking stick began to swell. It swelled up from the snake poison, don't you know, and it got thicker and thicker and longer and longer until pretty soon it was the size of a log.

It soon got so heavy that Cy couldn't carry it any more and he had to leave it out there in the field, still swelling. He ran to the barn and quick got the horses and some chain. When he come back that walking stick was swelled up bigger than a grand piano.

He hitched the chain around it, though, and had the horses drag it down the road to Butler, hurrying the team along so as to get there while it was still light-weight enough for them to tug it. He went to Butler, of course, because that's where Old Man Reeder and his boys has their sawmill. He had the Reeders saw up that walking stick into boards:

two-by-fours,

and joists,

and beams,

and ridgepoles,

and siding,
and shingles,
and little fancy louver doors.

And they took all those boards back home and built an entire *barn* out of them.

But it was not a successful experiment. No, sir, it did not pan out.

Because no sooner had they finished building this great barn when here up from the west comes one of these terrible Richland County thunderstorms. I don't know if you have storms where you live that are anything like the thunderstorms that people are used to in Richland County, Ashland County and the portions of other counties that make up the Mohican Country. So I don't know if you know what that new barn was up against.

First, folks see these great big angry purple clouds in the west, and they hear those clouds rumble as they bang against one another. Then the wind kicks up something fierce. I'll tell you, you know you're in trouble when you see a flock of ducks *flying backwards!* Why sure! They *have* to do that! It's the only way they have of keeping *sand* out of their eyes. Sometimes the wind gets to blowing so hard that it'll suck a well, sixty feet deep, right up out of the ground! Just like a straw being pulled out of a milkshake. Zip! and up it comes. Now what are you going to do with a well, sixty feet deep, that's been sucked up out of the ground? Why, you turn it upside down and use it for a *silo,* of course. When the wind blows that hard, people have to walk sideways to keep from flying! Either that or sew thirty pounds of lead weights into the lining of their hats! One time, they say, the wind come on so hard that it blew the eastern border of Richland County almost to the Pennsylvania line. They had to send out a team of county engineers afterwards to gather it up on great cable spools and bring it back and tamp it down good so's it wouldn't ever happen again!

Well, that day the purple clouds rumbled and the wind kicked up and then the rain started to fall. Harder and harder it fell, coming down thicker than pitch forks and hammer handles. It finally got to raining so hard that people caught out in it had to jump into the river to keep from drowning!

Cy looked out of his kitchen window through the rain over toward the new barn he had just built, but he couldn't make it out. He figured it was on account of the poor visibility caused by all that rain coming down so hard. But after a while the rain let up and when he looked out his window again, he *still* couldn't make out the barn.

He went out onto his porch and here he come to find that the entire barn had flat-out *disappeared.*

What happened? Simple. Like they say, hind-sight is twenty-twenty. The rain had washed all the snake poison *out* of those boards, don't you know, and they had all shrunk back down to their original size. When Cy went over to where that great barn had been, there was nothing left but a little pile of toothpicks, popsicle sticks and tongue depressors!

But Cy was always quick to see the silver lining.

"It was a good thing," Cy observed, "that we hadn't put any livestock in that barn or else they all would of been squeezed to death!"

A Few More Snakey Stories

Another time Cy was out walking around when he heard away off in the distance a rustling in the leaves on the forest floor. "Snakes!" he thought, and he was, as some people say in Richland County, "right as two rabbits."

He stalked up slow and easy to where that rustling sound was coming from and he lifted the leaves real careful with his walking stick, taking care to stand back at as far a distance as he could manage.

He peered under those leaves and it was snakes all right—*two of them!* They seemed to be having an argument. They hissed and spluttered at one another and circled round and round like two high school wrestlers, each one looking for a chance to grab at the other one.

Well, one of them suddenly made a lunge and clamped its jaws down tight on the other one's tail. Then, darned if the *other* snake didn't whip around, slick as a whistle, and snap onto the first one's tail.

And there they were, each snake with its jaws clamped down on the other's tail. Seeing that this was no particular advantage to him, the first snake began to chaw his way up the other snake's tail, chewing up and swallowing more and more of it into his mouth. And the other snake, not to be outdone, commenced to do the same.

The two snakes formed a circle now. And, as each one worked its way up the other's tail, the circle got smaller and smaller. Soon it was no bigger around than a wagon wheel. Then it was no bigger around than a barrel hoop. Next, it was no bigger around than a medium-sized pumpkin. When that circular pair of snakes got no bigger around than a hatband, Cy considered whether he ought to somehow knock both those snakes dead with his walking stick and use 'em for just that—a decorative hatband.

But before he could make up his mind, that circle got even smaller 'til it wasn't any bigger around than a coffee cup. Then it tightened up to the size of a walnut. The last glimpse Cy had of those two encircled snakes, the both of them combined weren't no bigger than a wedding ring.

Then, all of sudden, pop! They were entirely gone, vanished, disappeared—*because each snake had gone and eaten the other one right up!*

Now this is unusual behavior in snakes, to be sure. But a lot of the animals out to Wildcat Hollow behave in unusual ways.

Then too, there's a lot of animals live out to Wildcat Hollow that are unusual themselves. Some of them aren't generally known to most folks. Not that the animals can't be found anywhere else. No, most of the really unusual ones are actually common enough elsewhere, it's just that people don't seem to possess sufficient powers of observation to *notice* them.

Take snow snakes for an example. I feel safe in asserting that

very few people who read this book will be able to truthfully claim that they have ever actually *seen* a snow snake. Yet I feel equally safe in asserting that a great many of you will have seen *evidence* of where a snow snake has been—it's just that you didn't know what you were looking at.

Next time you're out walking on a winter's day, keep a sharp eye out. Look about you carefully and, if you're lucky and you know what you're looking for, sometimes you'll see, along the sidewalk or out in the woods, there in a white drift of snow...

a little, yellow hole.

That's where a snow snake lives!

But they're very timid creatures. Downright shy and reclusive! You can stand outside of one of those holes for the longest time and you'll never see one come out.

She painted the prettiest, most delicate spider web....

Cy's Remarkable Children

*All parents tell stories about their children...the
funny things they say, their amazing feats, their
endearing gestures, the little games they invent,
the imaginary worlds they inhabit.*

*Cy told stories about his children, too. For some
odd reason, though, Cy's stories about his own
children came out sounding like Tall Tales.
Maybe telling "whoppers" had become such a
habit that he didn't think twice about it. Or
maybe he just figured nobody would believe him
anyway, so why not have some fun?*

Daughter Nell

Cy Gatton had a daughter and her name was Nell.

Nell had her father's eye for Nature but she also possessed something he didn't have: a natural-born gift with a paint brush. She could mix up colors and dab them onto a canvas so as to make the prettiest pictures you ever saw.

The family first noticed this gift of Nell's when she was still just a little girl. The notice they took come about, strange to tell, on account of what Cy always referred to—even in his seventies—as his "premature balditude."

Cy was bald as a billiard ball. He said he was bald for the same reason you can't grow grass on a busy street. All those thoughts moving around in his head! It's only fair to add that his wife, Etta Pearl, would sometimes comment that you also can't grow grass out of concrete.

But, anyway, one of the consequences of his being bald was that the flies would be attracted to the smooth, shiny surface of his cranium. They would land on his bald head, two or three at a time, to socialize and gossip and this, that and the other. Of course, this bothered Cy considerably. He'd swat at those flies and wave his hands and curse and swear against them.

Now little Nell, when she was just a little mite of a thing, sweet and pretty as she could be, took notice of all the fuss and fume that was occasioned by these flies landing on Cy's bald head. And she had an idea of what to do about it, to give her father some relief from the pests. She went in to the kitchen and got a bottle of ink out of a drawer. Then she gathered up some cat hairs off the corner of the floor and rolled them together with a dab of glue until she had made the tiniest and finest little paint brush you ever set eyes on.

Then she got her Pa to kneel down on all fours and keep his nose to the ground and hold still 'til she was done. You know what

she did? She took that brush and that ink and she painted right onto his bald head the prettiest, most delicate spider web you can imagine. It grew up out of his eyebrows and stretched off symmetrically in all directions until it was lost in the fringe of hair he still had around the sides. The strands of that painted-on spider's web were so fine that you could hardly make them out.

But the flies made them out, all right—and, as everybody knows, a fly won't go anywhere near a spider's web if he can help it.

So from that day on, Cy had no more trouble with flies landing on his head.

As Nell got older, her gift with a paint brush got to be more and more skillful and astonishing. People thought Nell's pictures were just wonderful, but Nell herself was never satisfied. She'd struggle and fuss over her pictures, trying to get every detail just right. But somehow, no matter how good they seemed to everybody else, Nell would sigh and say, "Maybe I'll do better next time."

One time, Nell painted a fine painting of a boy holding a bunch of grapes. It was something to see, all right, and when she was done with it, Nell took it out into the yard so that the family could view the painting in the full blaze of daylight. She leaned it up against the porch railing and the family stepped out into the yard a few paces to behold this glorious new work of art.

It truly *was* amazingly realistic. The twinkle in that boy's eyes, the smile on his lips, the way his collar was kerflummoxed back just the way it would be on a hot day—why, you'd almost have sworn it was a tinted photograph. And the grapes! There was a great, glistening bunch of them hanging from that boy's grasp and it made the family's mouths water just to look at them.

The grapes, in fact, were so realistic that before anybody knew what was happening a couple of birds swooped down out of the sky and started pecking at them. For a second or two, the family was struck stone-still by the sight of that! Then they all run forward and shooed the birds away. And *then* they commenced to proclaim Nell the greatest painter of this or any other time!

"Nell!" they said, "You've done it! You've painted the most realistic paintin' ever seen! Your grapes was so real, you even

fooled the birds!"

But Nell was disappointed. "No," she said. "I'm a failure as a painter."

"What do you *mean,* girl?" Cy burst out, and his tone of surprise expressed the feelings shared by the whole family.

"Why, don't you see, Pa?" Nell said. "If I had painted the boy the way I *wanted* to paint him, he'd of scared the birds away!"

Another time Nell decided to paint a picture of a dog. She determined that this painting was to be her greatest work, her masterpiece. She determined that she would not quit working on it until it pleased her. She made up her mind in advance that this was to be the most realistic painting she ever made and if her keen eye detected even one tiny brush stroke that was false, she'd work it over and over and over until it was right and just suited her.

So she rolled up her sleeves and got to work. She painted at that painting all day long every day, week after week.

Say, that dog just got more and more realistic. After Nell had worked on it for a solid month, the family would creep into her sunny little painting room just to admire it. It was *so* realistic! You could see every whisker poking out from that dog's snout just as plain as day. You could see the gleam on that dog's molars. But still Nell was not satisfied.

She worked and she worked and the months passed by. All the time that dog became ever more realistic.

Finally the great moment arrived. Nell made one last deft stroke of the brush, stepped back to examine her work and pronounced herself satisfied.

She turned away from the painting to clean her brushes— *AND THE DOG BIT HER!*

The Story of Earl's Eyes

*C*y always aspired to be a good parent to his children, cost what it might in resources and time.

It's a well-known fact that, unlike bear cubs, children most generally possess a set of gifts and values, some which are the same and some of which are different from those of their parents. Cy's daughter Nell loved Nature and she could paint. Cy loved Nature but he couldn't draw a straight line. Cy's son Earl loved to figure out how things work and had a natural-born mechanical bent. Cy loved to figure out how things work but he didn't give a hoot about mechanics.

Cy never even learned to drive a car! On Saturdays, he'd just hitch the horse up to the wagon, same as he had always done, and wind slowly along Garber Road 'til he come to Bellville.

One Saturday in June, he was just ready to set off on his weekly re-supplying errand "over town" when his son Earl comes up.

"Where you off to, Pa?" asks Earl.

"Earl, I'm goin' over town same as I always do on Saturdays," Cy says. "You want-a come along?"

The boy said, "Sure!" and he hopped up onto the wagon seat alongside his Pa. They rode along together up to the top of Garber Road. Ah, there's not a prettier road in the whole of the Buckeye State than Garber Road. From up there you get a majestic view of the whole spacious Clear Fork Valley. You see what a lovely place this old earth truly is. You look down from up there and you can't help but wonder how anybody living in such a beautiful place could ever be anxious or sad. Cy was just drinking it all in, like he always did, glorying in the beauty he was so quick to see all around him.

"Just look at those *clouds*, Earl!" he'd say. "Ain't they beautiful now, all puffy and floatin' along so stately-like. How far off do you suppose that one is over there? Ain't it a funny thing that you never

can be sure how far off a cloud is? How far off is some tree? Oh, a mile or two. How far off is a hill?—five or six miles? But a *cloud?* Who can say how far off a cloud is? And we'll live our whole life never knowin', will we, Earl...Earl?"

The boy had not been paying the slightest attention to his Pa's rhapsody. You see, Earl had reached an age when he was interested in what you might call Practical Physics, Mechanical Sciences, How Man-made Things Are Put Together, and so on. Here he was, riding along through the most beautiful countryside in the world on the most beautiful day of summer, and all he wanted to look at was the wheels going round and round on that wagon. He'd crane his neck over sideways and study and study those wheels as they went round.

Amazing it was, to him, how a wheel worked, the way each spoke bore its share of the weight, but only for a moment...the miraculous hub of power that was represented by the axle...the ancientness of this greatest of all human inventions. Who had made the first wheel? Earl wondered what sort of person that inventor was. Someone like himself, he thought, for sure. Someone whose Pa probably went on windbagging about the beauties of Nature when all a body wanted to do was study how things worked in the world and how they might be made to work better.

Earl just kept right on staring at the wheel as it went round and round. Cy was sufficiently savvy about his audiences to know when he wasn't getting through, but pretended to take no notice of Earl's ignoring him. He just kept right on orating about the clouds and the trees and the birds and the hills, all the way into town.

It wasn't until they pulled up in front of the drug store and Cy went to hitch the horses that he noticed something had gone wrong with Earl. From staring at that wagon wheel going round and round, the boy's eyes had become *totally crossed!* His two eyeballs were so crisscrossed that his pupils was practically having a staring contest at each other across the ridge of his nose!

. And nothing would make them eyeballs go back right again. Oh, Cy tried everything he could think of. He shook Earl by the shoulders. He knocked him in the forehead with the heels of both

hands. He held him upside down by his ankles and shook him up and down—but nothing would do the trick. Though he took a dim view of "doctorin'" he got Earl to the doctor, who promptly pronounced the boy's eyes ruined for life and beyond the hope of modern medicine to cure.

Cy was just fit to be tied. He didn't know whether to yell at the boy or comfort him. Such a stupid thing to do, watching that wheel go round and round all the way into town like that! And yet he felt so sorry for the boy.

Then he thought of Etta Pearl. What was he going to tell the boy's mother? Now there was a thought. She'd blame *him*, of course.

He was "over town" now, though, and so he went through the motions of doing his errands, resupplying off a long list he'd prepared. It was a task that usually give him great pleasure. "Where on earth can you see more colors all clustered together or a collection of things gathered from a wider range of remote and exotic places than in a common grocery store?" he used to ask. But this time his heart wasn't in it. All he could think about was the boy's eyes being ruined for life, crossed the way they was.

So after he had made his rounds, it was with a heavy heart that he led the poor boy back over to the wagon and helped him up onto the wagon seat. Cy got up on the seat himself then, and he had just took the reins in his hands when it suddenly come to him what was needed to undo them crossed eyes of Earl's!

"Earl!" he shouted out. "By ziggety, you wanted to look at that wheel all the way into town, well, now you're going to *look at it all the way back!*" And with one hand Cy held Earl by the neck, keeping the boy's nose pointed down at that wheel, while with his other hand on the reins, he *backed up that wagon* all the way back up Garber Road until they got home.

And when they got back to home—what do you think?—the boy's eyes was *totally straightened out again!*

He stopped running and stuck out his fist.

Astonishing Adventures

Don't you hate to see the pages lessen in a book you love? I hope you're loving this book so much that you're wishing it would just go on and on. And it would, too, if it weren't for the silly notion that books must come to an end!

But our book isn't quite over yet, though this is Cy's last chapter. In it, bears, squirrels, snakes and shooters all take a final bow. And the entire Clear Fork Valley turns out to witness the dramatic recovery of the Reverend Hassenflue's false teeth!

Cy and the Bear

Cy's parental instincts were powerful and he loved and admired his children. He tried hard to strike just the right balance between loving them for exactly who they were and nurturing them along in the right direction.

Cy respected what he considered proper parenting wherever he encountered it and, of course, proper parenting is one of the lessons of Nature. "If there is one thing Mother Nature knows," Cy used to say, "it's how to raise up her children. She's all the time tuggin' and pushin' for every living thing to fulfill its destiny, and she's rootin' for us, too! just as hard as she does for all the rest."

Cy really believed this. He saw it at work with his own family and he saw it at work with the families of the forest and field. There was one time in particular...

He was out walking one day in the woods away back behind Wildcat Hollow when he heard a funny, little high-pitched squealy sort of a sound.

He cocked his ear and he listened hard until he could determine the direction that sound was coming from. It certainly was a *funny* sound—and I don't mean "funny: Ha, ha!" I mean "funny: Sheesh!"

It was a sound that Cy could never remember having heard before.

He held his hand to his ear and crept about the woods for a while until he narrowed down the direction of that sound. Following toward it, he drew closer and closer to a big old hollow tree until there was no doubt about it. That squealy sound was a-coming from inside that tree.

Now the tree had a man-sized hole in it about eight feet off the ground so Cy reached up and grabbed with both hands onto the bottom scoop of that hole. Then he pulled himself up until he could look down inside the tree, and what do you think he saw?

It was three little *baby bear cubs* that were making that

squealy sound. Right away Cy thought of the stories he had heard from his Grampa Isaac. It made him so happy the tears sprang to his eyes. "Bears! Bears! They've come back home to Richland County!" He could hardly believe it.

Well, of course, he climbed right on down in there and started playing with those cubs. Oh, it was great fun! He scratched their ears and tugged on their tails and tickled them under their chins and rolled them around and around like three little furry bowling balls. He was having a big time with those bear cubs, unmindful of all else and glad to the brink of insanity—when all of a sudden, just like that, it seemed like the lights went out inside that hollow tree and it was as black as Egypt!

He wondered what was going on and he quick looked up. In the dim light that was left he saw what it was—it was the Mama Bear, a-coming home to her cubs and not knowing there was any such thing as a *man* inside the big old hollow tree she called home. She was a-lowering herself down, hind-end first, coming closer and closer, and Cy knew he was in trouble.

He looked around to see if there was any other way out, but there were no side passages or tunnels. The only way out was the way he had come in and there was no sliding past her. That Mama Bear fairly plugged the hollow tree shut as she lowered herself down and down and down.

Another couple of seconds and she'd be right on top of him! Cy knew he had to come up with something quick. Well, he strained his brain and suddenly it come to him—an idea!

He quick reached in his pocket and pulled out his pocket-knife. He opened up the smallest little blade he had on that knife. And when the bear come down almost on top of him, why, he grabbed a hold of her tail with his left hand and with his right hand he took that pocketknife and give her a sharp little jab.

Rrrroarrrrr! She *burst* out of that hollow tree like a cannon ball coming out of the mouth of a cannon and she took off running through the forest as fast as she could go. This would have been just fine with Cy except for the fact that he found he was still a-hanging on to her tail! In all the excitement, he'd forgot to let go.

She didn't go far before she stopped running and looked

around behind her. And when she come to find that there was nobody back there but a little Cy Gatton man, a-hanging onto her tail, *was she mad!*

She took off after him and he had to run as fast as his legs could carry him to stay just ahead of her snapping jaws. He was pretty fast in those days, but he wasn't fast enough to outrun a furious Mama Bear. He ran uphill and the bear was gaining on him. He ran downhill and still the bear was gaining on him. He leapt over streams and rocks and fallen trees and the bear was right behind him. He could feel her hot breath on his neck— hhhah! hhhah! hhhah!

He knew he had to think of something quick, so once again he strained his brain—and all of sudden it come to him what he had to do.

He *stopped* running and stuck out his fist, with his knuckles turned right toward that bear. Now the bear wasn't looking for anything like this and what with her coming on full speed like that, why, before she knew what was happening, Cy stuck his fist right on in past her white, shiny teeth; he reached right on in past her pink slimy tongue; he reached clear on down into the dark inside of her until he grabbed a hold of her tail *on the inside* and then he give a mighty YANK!

And he *turned* that bear *inside out!*

Well, as soon as he had done that, Cy turned heel and ran home as hard as he could.

It took that Mama Bear a good half hour to get herself turned right-side out again. She had to be mighty careful doing it, too, on account of when all her fur passed *through* herself like that, why, she pert-near *tickled* herself to death! But when she did get herself turned right-side out again, she went right back to her home in that hollow tree, where her three little baby bear cubs were waiting for her. They were just fine. Cy took care to stay clear of that part of the woods, only peeking in on the family from a safe distance once in a great while. Old Mama Bear raised up her young'uns and when she judged they were old enough, she turned them loose in the woods away back behind Wildcat Hollow. And that's where they live to this day.

Cy Takes Earl Squirrel Hunting

Cy was mighty glad he'd gotten Earl's cross-eyed condition corrected, because he knew Earl would never make a squirrel hunter without a sharp eye.

This got Cy to thinking and he realized that Earl was already well past the age Cy himself had been the first time *he* had gone squirrel hunting. It was high time to introduce the boy to the mysteries of the ancient art. So the next day Cy took his son Earl out squirrel hunting.

That summer Cy taught Earl all he knew about the craft—and that was a considerable body of knowledge.

Some of Cy's tricks were a bit unconventional, as you can imagine. For one thing, he always carried *salt* with him when he went squirrel hunting. He'd mix a good tablespoon of salt in with his shot—he said it saved him having to salt the meat later on when the time come to eat it.

Well, it was getting along toward evening on Earl's first day out and they'd used up all their shells. All Cy had left was some black powder—which isn't of much use without a bullet—when they spotted five squirrels sitting in a row on a tree limb.

Cy saw those squirrels and he heaved a sigh. Then suddenly he remembered the story his Grampa Isaac had told him about that diamond-studded ramrod he had fashioned for himself. Cy loaded his rifle with a triple charge of powder and then let the ramrod slide all the way down the barrel. "Earl," Cy said, "You just watch me nail all five of them squirrels with a single shot!"

Then Cy went prowling around in the woods while the five squirrels just sat there, taking no notice.

When he had the angle just right, he took careful aim and fired—ka-boom!

That ramrod flew through the air and passed through all five of those squirrels like so much good advice from loving parents to their children—

in one ear and out the other,
and in one ear and out the other,
and in one ear and out the other,
and in one ear and out the other,
and in one ear and out the other!

Then Cy went up and retrieved his ramrod in full view of his son's astonished gaze. Cy let Earl carry home the trophy, five squirrels all hanging from that ramrod. Earl didn't say much, but Cy knew he was impressed. "Ah!" Cy thought. "A man likes to look good in front of his children!"

Cy's Elite Rifle Club

When Cy judged that Earl had mastered the craft of squirrel hunting, the two of them got together all the crack shots of the Clear Fork Valley, young and old alike, and formed them into a club. They called it The Elite Rifle Club.

All the members were great shooters—in fact, they were just about the best shots as ever was to be found anywhere.

The sole membership requirement consisted of a pretty tricky test.

Cy would take out the bung from the side of a fifty-gallon cider barrel and then send the barrel rolling down the hill in front of his house. It would get to rolling faster and faster until it got to where you could hardly see the bung hole go flying around and around.

The test was to wait until the barrel got to rolling full speed and then the hopeful candidate for membership in the Elite Rifle Club had to shoot a bullet *through* the bung hole of the barrel. He had to calculate the shot so that when the bullet *left* the barrel, it came out of that same bung hole it had gone *into!*

It was a tricky shot to make, but it was easy enough to see whether or not the prospective new member had met the challenge. All you had to do was examine the barrel afterwards. If it still had but the one hole in it—the bung hole, that is—and no *other* holes, why then it was plain to see that the challenge had been met. That meant the Elite Rifle Club had just swelled its membership roles by the number one.

It was a good way to test marksmanship as well as to preserve the barrels for the purpose of storing next year's cider.

Double-layered Bull's Hide Hip Boots

Many have wondered why The Elite Rifle Club didn't turn its powers to the benefit of the public by shooting snakes instead of squirrels. "Squirrels don't harm nobody, after all," they'd say, "while snakes is bothersome, scaring the little children and all!"

Cy had to admit that they had a point. But somehow Cy and the other members of the E.R.C. just couldn't bring themselves to shoot a snake. Not that they felt any affection for the loathsome creatures—far from it! But it seemed unmanly somehow to kill a snake from such a distance and with a rifle.

Besides, Cy had long since discovered a far better way of keeping the snake population under control.

Before I tell you about that, I want to say something right out straight. You might get the idea from these stories that the only thing Cy had to do with his time was to hang around his property, playing it safe, taking no chances, having a mild little local adventure now and again, and then telling all about it to anybody who'd listen.

Well, if that is what you think, then you are mistaken.

Cy was a hard-working man. He had his farm to look after and

farming is no small task, then or now. Nobody works harder or
is a bigger gambler than a farmer. Cy worked hard at farming all
of his long life, hoping for the right amount of rain and the right
amount of sunshine. For most of that time the farm belonged to
him and the stakes were high. Of course when he was a boy the
farm still belonged to his Grandpa Isaac. Then as time went by the
property was passed on to his father and finally to him. But even

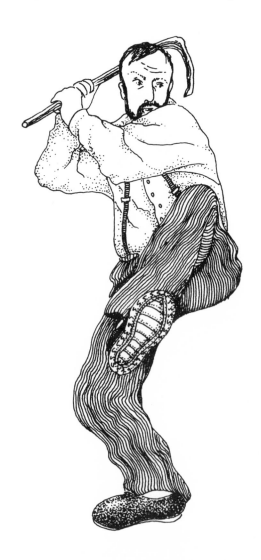

as a boy, working on land that belonged to his grandpa, Cy had to work hard.

He was out in the fields working hard one day at mowing. I'm not talking about mowing with a lawn mower or a tractor. In those days, people mowed by the strength of their arms, swinging great big farm tools called mowing scythes. These tools had a curved wooden helve, or handle, that you grabbed onto in two different places. The helve was attached to a three-foot-long blade that was razor-sharp as you'll recall from the story about the World's Fastest Hunting Dog. Those mowing scythes were *heavy* and swinging them back and forth to cut hay was a job that required a lot of strength.

Cy had the strength for the job, all right, but the thing that troubled *him* was the *snakes*. In those days the snakes out there in the fields were *thick*. Cy wouldn't have minded one or two of them now and again but when it got to the point where he had to spend more than half his time stepping over snakes and jumping out of the way of snakes and fighting off snakes he decided that the time had come to *do* something about the problem.

He pondered on it, strained his brain, and, as usual, it wasn't long before an idea come to him. What he needed, he figured, was some kind of protection from the snakes. He needed some kind of armor, you might say, to fit around his legs and thighs so's he could go on about his mowing work and give the snakes no thought.

But how was a poor farm boy going to come up with leg armor?

Then he happened to remember a family heirloom, a possession that had belonged to his Grandpa Isaac and had been almost as much prized by the old pioneer as his diamond-studded ramrod. It was a pair of double-layered, bull's hide hip boots that his Grampa Isaac had used for fishing.

Well, he dug out those hip boots from the attic and he slipped them on. Then back out to the field he went.

Ha! No trouble with snakes now! He'd just mow and mow and those snakes would come up to him and spring at him and sink their fangs right into those double-layered bull's hide hip boots.

And those boots bein' as thick as they were, you see, why, the snakes couldn't never penetrate anywhere *near* deep enough to come close to Cy's flesh. So he was safe from the creatures, so long as he wore those double-layered bull's hide hip boots.

But now he had a *new* problem. The snakes would attack and sink their fangs in and then they couldn't get them back out. So there they'd be, stuck, with their fangs bit in deep and their long waggly tails a-flip-flopping all around. Cy didn't mind two or three of them hanging on that way, but after an hour or two here he was with forty or fifty snakes, all of them with their teeth sunk in deep and all of them with their tails waggling all around.

The weight of all those snakes got to be downright cumbersome!

What was he going to do?

He pondered a bit and then it come to him. He had the solution right close to hand in that mowing scythe. He aimed that razor-sharp blade just so and he swept the edge of it right up across his boots, from the ankles to the hips, shaving his legs, you might say. He sliced off those snake-heads right at the neck.

This technique would free him up for another hour or so until he'd collected another half a hundred snakes and then, of course, he had to do it again and then later on again after that. Still, it was a major improvement over spending all that energy dodging the snakes and it seemed a more manly way of dispensing with them than shooting would have been. Cheaper, too, there being no bullets or gunpowder involved.

At the end of the day, when Cy walked back to the house, those double-layered bull's hide hip boots were covered thick with snake heads from belt buckle to heel.

And just imagine young Cy's satisfaction that evening, sitting by the fire, thinking back on a good day's work, crossing his legs and sitting back in full view of his younger brothers, plucking out those snake heads one at a time, tossing them into the fire and listening to them *sizzle!* Hoo-hah!

Cy Saves the Preacher's False Teeth

What a store of memories old Cy Gatton had! A whole library of stories to carry around with him right in his head! True stories, partly true stories, and stories with hardly any truth in them whatsoever. What a collection!

And most all of them set in scenes right close to hand, right there in the Mohican Country, in southern Richland County, in the Clear Fork Valley, out to Wildcat Hollow, over town to Bellville or down to the swinging bridge. And all among neighbors, guests and friends.

The swinging bridge, as you'll recall, was where Cy first met (and was later tricked into thinking he'd lost) his remarkable pet catfish. That bridge is still fondly remembered by many older people of the area. As young sweethearts, they would stroll across it and meander up and down the shady shores of the gentle little river that flowed beneath it. It was the scene of many a social gathering. Family reunions, ice cream socials, high school class reunions and church picnics all assembled there regularly.

The swinging bridge and the river under and alongside it had been the scene of one of Cy's earliest heroics. It was not exactly an adventure, but it made folks sit up and take notice of him, which was *always* just fine with Cy Gatton.

It happened on the occasion of the annual Sunday School Picnic. All the families of the Clear Fork Valley had gathered for the big event. The Leedys, the Oysters, the Bells, the Durbins, the Millers, the Garbers, the Divelbisses, the Swanks, the Reeders, the Hizeys, the Gattons and all the rest. And, of course, the preacher who was ministering to the valley at the time was there as well, a large man, the Reverend Dr. Xenophon Hassenflue. The men set boards across sawhorses and the women covered them (the sawhorses, that is) with red-and-white checkered tablecloths. Then they set out the food and you should have *seen* the spread.

Say! There was fried chicken and sliced tomatoes and corn on

the cob and fried chicken and deviled eggs and watermelon pickle and fried chicken and scalloped potatoes and green bean casserole and fried chicken and homemade egg noodles and creamed peas and onions and fried chicken and corn bread and dinner rolls and fried chicken and lemon pie and chocolate cake and fried chicken and lemonade and hot coffee and fried chicken...because, you see, the Reverend Dr. Hassenflue *loved* fried chicken. And all the good women would try and outdo each other to see if they could get the preacher to pronounce *theirs* the best! But Rev. Hassenflue, he was far too smart to do that. He'd go round and sample each dish, making sure to leave not a one untouched, and he loquaciously expressed his admiration for the fried chickens, one and all. But he wisely took care never to put any one of them ahead of the rest.

Well, after everybody had eaten all they could hold, there was games and fun of all sorts and then after a while things calmed down. The old people sat in the shade fanning themselves and the young people strolled up and down in pairs all enthralled with each other and the children went out to wade and splash in the river, cooling themselves. The Rev. Xen. Hassenflue, D.D., went up onto the swinging bridge and stood right in the middle of it. It was a steep slope uphill from either side of the Rev. X.H., the bridge straining under his weight. As he put it, the Lord had bestowed upon him the gift of corpulence.

He was leaning over the side of the bridge, grasping the cable in his hands and sincerely enjoying the frolicsome aquatic cavortings of what he called "the lambs of his flock" when all of a sudden...well, no one ever did learn the cause of it. Maybe it might have been one of the hairs of his mustache that somehow kind of corkscrewed and curlicued its way up into his nose. But anyhow, whatever the cause, all of a sudden he felt overcome with an overpowering and irresistible desire to sneeze. He sucked in quick all the air he could hold beneath those great paps of his and then he cut loose with a mighty *whoooooop!*

The sound of that sneeze went echoing down the valley. And the sound of that sneeze was followed by the sound of something going—*plop*—right into the water.

It was the preacher's false teeth! Xenophon Hassenflue had

sneezed so hard that his false teeth had gone *flying* out of his mouth and landed with a *bloop*—right in the river.

Now Cy and all the other kids that was wading in the water had looked up as soon as the preacher let out that mighty sneeze. All of them had seen the false teeth land in the water. Naturally, every one of them saw just as clearly that Fate or Destiny or Providence, whatever you want to call it, had presented them with the chance to become the Hero of the Day by retrieving the preacher's false teeth!

So most all the kids started a-rooting down into the water, closing their eyes and getting their shirts and smocks wet, while they groped about on the bottom of the river, hoping to come upon those false teeth.

But Cy didn't waste no time with that foolishness. No, sir! Even *then* he was smarter than that. What he did was, he run over to the tables alongside the river, where the leftover food was. And he grabbed the biggest, greasiest leg of chicken he could find.

Then he took a piece of twine and tied one end of it around that chicken leg and he run up onto the swinging bridge, right next to the preacher. He lowered that twine-bound chicken leg down into the water. You see, that preacher had loved fried chicken so much for so long, that when that chicken leg came a-floating by those chompers, why they made a *GRAB* at it—and Cy *yanked* 'em right up out of the water!

And *that* was how he saved the preacher's false teeth.

Many years later, when Cy felt the winter coldness an old man sometimes feels, when he needed to warm himself from the inside with good memories, he would think back on how it had been on that happy day when he had rescued the pastoral dentures— the Rev. Hassenflue embarrassed but so grateful, his parents so proud, and him shining in front of his brothers and all the other kids, a regular hero.

A herd of Shredded Wheats was playing leapfrog.

Is The Tall Tale Dead? Judge for Yourself

Farmers used to just cut hay with a scythe and arrange it in stacks. Then came a machine that made square bales held together with binder twine. More recently, someone invented a machine that makes round bales.

Because round bales hadn't been invented in Cy Gatton's day, this is a modern story. But it is just as creative as the ones the old-timers told. Cy would have been proud to tell it.

*T*he annual Farm Bureau banquet was over, people were leaving. I, the guest speaker, was gathering up my things and saying my thanks and goodbyes when I became aware of him standing in front of me.

He was a grizzled old farmer with thick gray hair and a style of spectacles that I used to see older folks wear when I was a boy, back in the fifties.

"I enjoyed those Cy Gatton stories you told," he said. "Pretty amazing goings-on, over there in Richland County." He spoke in a flat, matter-of-fact way, but not without enthusiasm.

"'Course, we got a resource around here that nobody talks much about, the Shredded Wheat stud farms."

I wasn't sure I had heard him correctly.

"You've seen 'em," he said. "Big round things, look like they're made out of hay, standing around out in the fields?"

Then it hit me. "Oh!" I said. "You mean round bales."

"Some people call 'em that, but Shredded Wheats is what they are," he replied. He looked as dead serious as a man can look. "It's an animal like any other. If you get 'em when they're little, in the larva stage, the *veal,* you might call it, well, then they're young and tender. You can eat them for a breakfast cereal if you care to. Later on, as they grow larger, they get tougher and they're only fit for cattle fodder.

"You see 'em out in the fields grazing, big round things. Originally bred from a hybrid cross between the tumbleweed and the woolly worm, you know.

"They're slow to mature. You drive by a field of grass three feet high? They're in there, little Shredded Wheats, running all around on the ground like mice. And then, the next day, you drive by that same field and all the grass is gone, just like that! What's happened? Why, they've gone and *eaten* it all up! Suddenly reached what the ag professors call the 'pupa' stage. You see them, rectangular-shaped in this stage of their life, scattered all over a field where the day before there was nothing but grass.

Overnight, those little creatures will eat as much as fifty times their weight in grass. They'll nibble it right down to the ground and convert the intake to body parts!

"Then they're dormant for a while. Farmers don't have to chase 'em around much. A farmer'll just go over to one of 'em, pick it up and pile it onto a flatbed wagon along with the rest. Sometimes you see farmers driving a tractor slowly down the road, pulling a whole load of rectangular-shaped pupa-stage Shredded Wheats, stacked half-dozen high. Ever wonder what those farmers are doing? Why, they're taking those Shredded Wheats over to fresh pasture where they can graze some more and develop into the final, mature state, all big and round, what they call, like you said, round bales.

"Sometimes you see these 'round-baled' Shredded Wheats standing in a field, all of them solitary and apart, keeping away from each other. That means there's trouble in the herd, and none of 'em are speaking to one another. But that's unusual, actually. Most often you see 'em in the single-file herd formations they prefer...all lined up in a row and waiting for you to drive on by so's they can cross the road, one at a time, Indian style, the way they like to do.

"Shredded Wheat stud farmers are forming an association and they're going to start a Shredded Wheat Promotion & Research check-off program to raise money for marketing. They want to find new uses for their product. If you've tasted it as a breakfast cereal, I think you'll agree that human consumption should be way down toward the *bottom* of the list.

"Oh, yes, they're going to hire university researchers and scientists and whole teams of marketers. They're going to look into competing with the Brillo Pad and the makers of excelsior packaging material. And did you ever see in the big cities how they have these huge street-sweeping trucks? Pah! Those things are noisy and they pollute the air. Well, sir, there's some fellow down to the Ohio State Veterinary School has just about got some round-baled Shredded Wheats trained to do the same job. They make no noise, they're non-polluting and they *eat* the trash right up off the street. Convert the trash to body parts, don't you see? Talk about solid waste management!

"The American Society of Shredded Wheat Option-Buyers & Producers is going to hire Paul Harvey to go on the radio to announce their product as 'the only green meat,' just like he calls pork 'the other white meat.' Of course, Shredded Wheat isn't really green, but then pork isn't really white neither, truth be told.

"During mating season the Shredded Wheats go to pieces, just like everybody else. The farmers have to wrap them in that industrial-strength vinyl you've seen on 'em, comes in both white and black. They have to seal 'em up like that to keep 'em from reproducing. Why, if it weren't for those vinyl wrappings, this whole country would be nothing but wall-to-wall Shredded Wheat!"

And then he turned and was out the door before I could even thank him for telling me about this little-understood resource.

Since that night, I've driven thousands of miles on Ohio roads and highways. Whenever I pass a field of round bales I always look closely to see if I can catch them actually moving. Now and again, and usually around twilight, I've thought I glimpsed one of them twitch or shudder or scratch itself.

But I'm not completely certain.

A Note on Sources

Most of the stories Cy Gatton told about himself were already "old stories" when he told them. Many of his tall tales would have been well known to his listeners who had heard them from pioneer grandparents. Cy Gatton's invention of the character "Cy Gatton" was one storyteller's personal response to the receding memory of the days of the old Northwestern frontier. What made Cy's stories fresh and new were his straight-faced claims that the adventures recounted in these stories had actually happened to HIM. That he was able to do this without seeming egotistical or braggardly constitutes yet another testimony to his celebrated skill as a storyteller.

Cy pulled together his own collection of stories from a variety of sources. Using a local setting and adding a few deft twists and images, he pronounced himself the protagonist. In other words, the actual historic person Cy Gatton made his fictional character "Cy Gatton" the hero of an epic cycle of oft-told and well-loved American stories made to take place in north-central Ohio's Mohican Country. Thus, "Cy Gatton" became a figure who can take his place among the gallery of American folk heroes associated with specific regions of the country. The character he created is Ohio's answer to Paul Bunyan, Pecos Bill, Davy Crockett, Mike Fink and John Henry.

When I began to assemble the Cy Gatton stories I had heard from family, friends and neighbors, I realized that I did not have a sufficient supply of them to create a full evening's entertainment. So, like Cy before me, I drew on a number of sources: stories gathered from other storytellers I'd heard, and some gathered from books, too, such as Alvin Schwartz's *Whoppers: Tall Tales and Other Lies*. I first heard about beanholes and snow snakes from my Scoutmaster. Imagine my surprise afterwards

when older people came up to me and said they recalled Cy Gatton telling those very stories! Did I "swipe" those stories from storytellers and books or did the books and storytellers "swipe" them from other, earlier storytellers such as Cy?

The truth is that almost all of these stories have been floating around for hundreds of years, some even for thousands. The story I tell about Nell's painting of the boy holding a bunch of grapes comes down from ancient Greece. Grampa Isaac's miraculous hunting story dates back to the Middle Ages. We know for a fact that Cy Gatton actually did tell the stories about the tornado, the snakes that swallowed each other, the lantern in the tunnel, the unscrewing of the owl's head, the wintry woodpecker, the spider's web painted onto his bald head, the pet catfish and many others. But where did he get those stories? Is it accurate or fair to state that he "swiped" them?

Nobody "swiped" them from anybody. A more accurate way of saying it is that all stories are swiped from somewhere or other, a process that pre-dates even the ancient Greeks. Most scholars believe that Homer, if he or she even existed, merely assembled a lot of fragments from earlier times and strung them together brilliantly into The Iliad and The Odyssey. All of Chaucer's stories were already old when he put them into rhymed couplets in the Canterbury Tales. And very few, if any, of mighty Shakespeare's plots are original with him.

Still, Cy Gatton's use of specific local settings and actual historic personages has always prompted listeners to ponder where fact ceases and fancy begins. Perhaps it is helpful to recall how often this question has been deliberately raised in the best American literature.

American storytellers have always delighted in blurring the line that separates fact from fancy.

Where does fact cease and fancy begin in the stories Cy Gatton told (and which I now tell) about "Cy Gatton?" Who knows? Who cares? Let the question hover unanswered and accept the unsatisfied itch of curiosity for what it is: the chief-most tickle of the Tall Tale.

The Author

Nowadays, Rick Sowash earns his living as a full-time professional humorist, performing at schools, banquets, libraries, parks, festivals, colleges, conventions and theaters across America. 'Twas not always thus.

Prior to launching himself as an entertainer, he was in a different branch of show business—politics! He served his native Richland County, Ohio, as a county commissioner for four long years. He did not seek re-election. He refers to this experience as "death by a thousand wounds."

Of all things, arts administration was his springboard into the shark-infested waters of local politics. He had been the founding executive director of the Renaissance Theatre in Mansfield, Ohio, a 1,500-seat movie palace reborn under his leadership as a community center for the performing arts.

At various times he has also been a broadcaster for Columbus's public radio station WOSU-FM (classical music), a full-time church musician (Lutheran), and the co-developer with his wife, Jo, of a noted bed-and-breakfast country inn in Bellville, Ohio. At one point, he even enjoyed some colorful adventures while riding shotgun for five months on a beer truck (Stroh's).

He's more or less proud of all the twists and turns he's taken in his curious career, but he is far prouder of the music he writes. Rick Sowash is a composer of classical music, claiming to be "the only American composer ever elected to public office." He is a member of ASCAP and has 160 choral, chamber and orchestral works to his credit. These are published, performed, recorded and broadcast around the world.

For Rick Sowash composing is a serious and life-long pursuit, albeit a non-professional one. Hey, you can't support a family by writing classical music in rural Ohio—or anywhere else for that matter!

Most of all, Rick Sowash and his wife Jo are proud of their children—a daughter named Shenandoah Lee (after the song, the park and the Civil War general) and a son named John Chapman (after the Ohio folk-hero better known as Johnny Appleseed).

The Illustrator

Maureen O'Keefe's love of art began as a child with the beautifully colored pictures in her family's set of children's books. She was encouraged in art by her parents, who gave her permission to paint on her bedroom walls.

Her drawings are colorfully detailed and usually decorated with striking borders. Her early works used soft colors but she recently has begun using a more vibrant palette. Much of her work includes hidden symbols. Her use of line and dots give her work a lineal appeal.

Maureen O'Keefe's work has appeared in many shows in Ohio and Michigan, and her work is in private collections in Michigan, Ohio, Canada, Ireland and Australia. Her shows include a slide presentation of her drawing titled "Women of the Bible," which includes her own interpretive story about each picture. She continues to give this presentation to churches and women's groups.

Maureen O'Keefe's work tells a story, and when presenting it to groups, she relates the story within the picture. She especially enjoys telling her stories to children.

Before illustrating *Ripsnorting Whoppers!* her most recent work was the illustrations for *How the Children Stopped the Wars,* a children's book by Jan Wahl (Berkeley, CA: Tricycle Press, 1993).

We made this book.

Designers:
Gene Hite and Dean Kette, Principals
Design Communications, Inc.
Columbus, Ohio

Production:
Nancy Lee Nelson, Production Manager
UniGraphics
Bowling Green State University
Bowling Green, Ohio

Photography of Rick Sowash:
Barbara Vogel
Columbus, Ohio

Cover Separations:
Kim Cribb,
Customer Associate
SFC Graphics, Inc.
Toledo, Ohio

Book Manufacturer:
Linda Skrzypek,
Customer Service Representative
Thomson-Shore, Inc.
Dexter, Michigan

Colophon: Using text written in WordPerfect 5.1 on MS-DOS computers, UniGraphics composed the text of this book in Garamond on a Varityper 4300P PostScript imagesetter. The book is printed on 60-lb. Glatfelter Supple Opaque Recycled text paper.

Sources of pictures not otherwise credited: Page 2, Don Palm; page 135, James Bissland; page 139, Fred Martens.

Index

The Music of Rick Sowash

Rick Sowash is a well-known American composer whose music is published, performed, recorded and broadcast around the world.

"The compositions of Rick Sowash impressed me with their fresh spirit, sense of humor, and unmistakably American sound."—David M. Brin, Editor, *Strings*.

Recordings available are:

CD: *Rick Sowash: The Four Piano Trios,* featuring The Mirecourt Trio. "As American as apple pie."—*Opus* magazine.

CD: *Rick Sowash: Chamber Music with Clarinet,* featuring The Mirecourt Trio and clarinetist Craig Olzenak. "Cheerful, unpretentious, exuberant, and heart-felt, with a disarming freshness and innocence...soaring, folklike lyricism pervades Sowash's compositions."—Walter Simmons, *Fanfare* magazine.

CD: *20th Century Harpsichord Music,* Vol. 1, offers selections by seven modern composers including Sowash's "The Unicorn and Theme with 6 Variations" performed by Barbara Harbach.

CD: *20th Century Harpsichord Music,* Vol. 4, offers selections by eight modern composers including Sowash's "Harbachsichord Suite."

"Full of an uplifting joie de vivre...good tunes and unexpected developments...a joy and a delight...I can recommend [it] with enthusiasm."—*American Record Guide.*

CD & cassette tape: *Music for the Appalachian Trail* featuring the Shelburne Quartet playing Sowash's "Fantasia on 'Shenandoah'" along with other music celebrating the world's longest footpath.

"Attractive and pleasing to the ear."—*American Record Guide.*

Cassette tape: *Cape May Suite and A Little Breakfast Music* featuring The West End Chamber Ensemble. "Sweetly and simply tuneful, with an identifiably American flavor."—*Fanfare* magazine.

To order recordings, call Gasparo Records at
1-800-934-8821

Rick Sowash's choral music is published by Lawson & Gould Music Publishers; order by calling 1-212-247-3920. Sowash's chamber music is published by D.I. Music, 13 Bank Square, Wilmslow, Cheshire, SK9 1AN, England.

Ripsnorting Whoppers!
The Book

If you've enjoyed this book, you know others will, too. Why not order copies for them? *Ripsnorting Whoppers! Humor From America's Heartland* is a great gift for anyone who enjoys a good story. (Know anyone who doesn't?)

Ripsnorting Whoppers! is good reading for all ages, including older elementary school children as well as adults. Every year, author Rick Sowash tells his tales to over a hundred audiences, ranging from youngsters in school to senior citizens.

The book, as well as audio tape and video versions, are available in stores or directly from the publisher.

To order, call Gabriel's Horn Publishing Co. at:

1-800-235-4676

or use order blank at the end of this book.

Ripsnorting Whoppers!
The Audio Tape

Highlights from the book on a 60-minute audio cassette, read by the author. Rick Sowash draws on his experience as a radio broadcaster and storyteller to re-tell, as only he can, his own favorite stories from the book. Of special interest to commuters and the sight-impaired.

To order, call Gabriel's Horn Publishing Co. at
1-800-235-4676
or use order blank at the end of this book.

Ripsnorting Whoppers!
The Video

(originally released as "Cy Gatton & the Great American Whopper.")

A joyful, hilarious and captivating 60-minute video documentary on the life and stories of the Heartland folk hero-storyteller Cy Gatton. Produced in cooperation with WOUB Public Television in Athens, Ohio, this richly entertaining film features rare photos of Cy Gatton and the America he knew.

Glimpse a vanished turn-of-the-century way of life and savor Rick Sowash's re-tellings of Cy's best stories before a live audience. Includes many of the stories in the book, and some new ones as well.

To order, call Gabriel's Horn Publishing Co. at
1-800-235-4676
or use order blank at the end of this book.

Other Books of Interest
from
Gabriel's Horn

BOUNTIFUL OHIO, by James Hope and Susan Failor (1993). A celebration of the food and people of the state where America's Heartland begins. This 224-page book offers 163 down-home recipes, plus lore about Ohioans and their bountiful state. Generously illustrated with pictures both old and new. *Softcover:* $14.95; *hardcover:* $21.95; *signed and numbered limited first printing* (while supplies last): $39.95.

"A loving tribute to the state."—*The Cleveland Plain Dealer.* **"Stories readers will find fascinating."**—*The Columbus Dispatch.* **"You'll be hooked!** *Bountiful Ohio* **is one enjoyable read from beginning to end."**—*Northern Ohio Bibliophilic Society Newsletter.* **"The kind of book you will read again and again."**—*Cookbook Collectors' Exchange.*

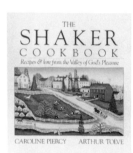

THE SHAKER COOKBOOK, Caroline Piercy and Arthur Tolve (1984). The latest revision of a classic, this 192-page book is filled with delicious, authentic recipes updated for modern convenience. And there's abundant lore and many sketches from the Shaker settlement where the Cleveland suburb of Shaker Heights is today. *Softcover:* $14.95.

"Hardy, simple, quaint recipes abound."—*Booklist.* **"The cookbook is beautifully illustrated...bits of Shaker lore and verse are sprinkled throughout."**—*Country Living.*

To order, call Gabriel's Horn Publishing Co. at
1-800-235-4676
or use order blank at the end of this book.

**To order books,
audio tapes
or videos,
use order form
on other side.**

Order Form for Books, Audio Tapes and Videos

This form may be copied

If the book, audio tape or video version of *Ripsnorting Whoppers! Humor from America's Heartland* isn't available at your favorite store, you may order directly from the publisher. Telephone 1-800-235-4676 or mail form and payment to:

Gabriel's Horn Publishing Co.
Department R
P.O. Box 141
Bowling Green, OH 43402

Quantity	Title and Edition	Price each	Total
_____	RIPSNORTING WHOPPERS! (soft)	$11.95	$ _____
_____	RIPSNORTING WHOPPERS! (hard)	$19.95	$ _____
_____	RIPSNORTING WHOPPERS! (audio)	$9.95	$ _____
_____	RIPSNORTING WHOPPERS! (video)	$24.95	$ _____
_____	BOUNTIFUL OHIO (soft)	$14.95	$ _____
_____	BOUNTIFUL OHIO (hard)	$21.95	$ _____
_____	BOUNTIFUL OHIO (limited)	$39.95	$ _____
_____	THE SHAKER COOKBOOK (soft)	$14.95	$ _____

UPS SHIPPING:
$3 first book, 50¢ each thereafter. $ _____

Ohio residents add 6% tax. $ _____

TOTAL AMOUNT ENCLOSED $ _____
Check or MasterCard/VISA acceptable.

Name _____

Street address _____

City _____ State _____ ZIP _____

Card no. _____ Expires _____